A MANUAL OF
HAND-MADE BOBBIN
LACE WORK

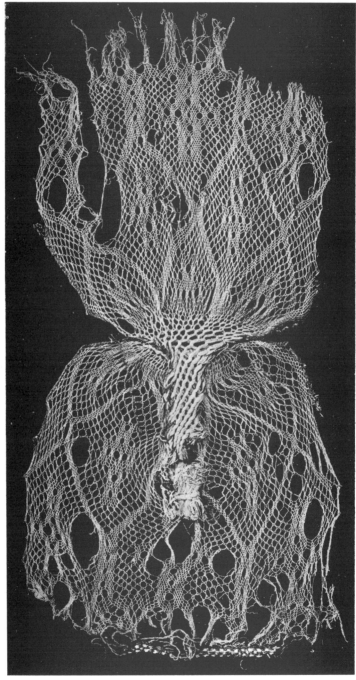

PLAITED WORK FROM AKHMIM (PANOPOLIS), UPPER EGYPT
VICTORIA AND ALBERT MUSEUM, 50—1891

[Frontispiece

A MANUAL OF
HAND–MADE BOBBIN
LACE WORK

By
MARGARET MAIDMENT
Cert. R.S.A.N., City and Guilds of London
(Full Technological Certificate for Embroidery and Allied Subjects)
Teacher of Lace-making at the Royal School of Needlework
Instructor in Embroidery and Lace-making at the
Battersea Polytechnic, London

B T Batsford Ltd,　London

First published 1931
This edition published 1983

ISBN 0 7134 3855 X

For technical reasons this edition has been printed in monochrome. Colour
distinction in the original edition has been kept by either shaded grey or solid
white

Printed and bound in Great Britain
by The Anchor Press Ltd, Tiptree, Essex
for the publishers
B T Batsford Ltd, 4 Fitzhardinge Street, London, W1H 0AH

FOREWORD

IT is stated that records are available of lace-like fabrics from the land of the Pharaohs, said to be of flax cloth with coloured threads, and patterns drawn and worked in geometric design. The crossing of one equal set of fibres or threads by another set at right angles may be considered as the source or constructive motive from which lace patterning was derived; thus we have elements of utility and necessity in the early woven fabrics, leading to the elements of design and ornamental effects and supplying the essential qualities for aesthetic expression in lace. Accepting this ancient form of ornamentation as a basis, the next step might be described as the enrichment along the edges of costumes; this consisted of small cords of plaited and twisted threads fastened in loops, of darning on net grounds and of drawn-thread work. From these types of early work lace is descended.

Needlepoints and pillow laces were first produced at the beginning of the sixteenth century. The two countries that claim to be the birthplace of these two classes of lace are Flanders and Italy. A considerable amount of literature on the art of lace-making has appeared, and some of the earliest, and perhaps the most important work on the subject, are the series of lace pattern books of sixteenth and seventeenth century examples by F. Vinciolo, published in 1587. France and England were not far behind Venice and Flanders in adopting lace.

The early efforts in lace-making in England were confined mainly to the humble endeavours of the peasantry living and working away from the advanced conditions of culture prevailing in cities and towns. Their lace work had no artistic pretensions, but it had a pleasing character which was free from affectations, and not the result of conscious effort. They could not boast any school of design, but as the work progressed motives of design from a higher strata of art are often discernible, and by degrees lace work acquired distinctive qualities in the various English counties such as Bedfordshire, Buckinghamshire and Devonshire. Machine-made lace was introduced towards the end of the eighteenth century, but it invariably lacks the peculiar individuality or style of hand-work: and while the machine can produce some remarkable imitations of hand-made laces of certain types, the finest and most elaborate of hand-made laces stand entirely alone, and machine reproductions of them are practically unobtainable.

The author of this book has a comprehensive and expert knowledge of lace technique, and she has dealt with the subject in an exhaustive and thoroughly practical manner. The methods of working, the clear and straightforward descriptions given in systematic progressive stages, and the large number of diagrams, should prove extremely useful to all lace workers. A revival in hand-made lace would be a national benefit. Lace-making, not long ago, was an industry that *did* bring regular remuneration to those engaged in it; it was essential then that well composed designs were produced for the use and guidance of the workers, and there are plenty of capable designers who can produce them to-day. Lace-making is largely a home or cottage industry, but there is no reason why self-supporting English lace schools should not become an accomplished fact.

W. G. PAULSON TOWNSEND.

April, 1931.

PREFACE

A FEW years ago, when I was giving a special course of lessons to some London County Council teachers, I tried the experiment of teaching by means of enlarged diagrams. Many of them worked with coloured threads. The result proved so satisfactory that I have ever since adopted the same plan in teaching students of Lace and Embroidery. They and others have repeatedly urged me to issue my diagrams in book form. It has given me the greatest pleasure to endeavour to carry out their wishes, and I can only hope that my effort will prove of benefit to the craft.

In describing the different kinds of bobbin lace made in England I have kept as far as possible to the methods used by the workers of the different counties. In lace as in some other industries continental workers follow different rules and yet attain the same result. I have used English names, as the technical terms in use on the Continent are often perplexing. As some stitches are known by various names in the different English counties, there is a danger of confusion, so in the description of each kind of lace, although I have given the name used by the local workers, I have also allowed the other name to appear in the general notes.

Stitches and fillings that are used in more than one kind of lace are described in that particular make in which they occur most frequently, but reference is also made to them in regard to other laces.

This is not intended as a book of patterns and designs, but it gives sufficient technical details of the stitches, and methods, to enable the worker to arrange her own patterns.

All the stitches and methods are obtained from reliable sources.

I have received much valuable assistance from many friends to whom I gratefully express my thanks, and especially to Mr. W. G. Paulson Townsend; Mr. Thomas Wright, of Olney, who has published a work called *The Romance of the Lace-pillow*, being the History of Lace Making as concerns principally the counties of Bucks, Beds, Northants, Hunts, Herts, and Oxon; Miss A. E. Tompkins, of the Battersea Polytechnic; and also the authorities of the Victoria and Albert Museum, to whom I have offered a number of the original diagrams for the use of students.

MARGARET MAIDMENT.

CONTENTS

PAGE

FOREWORD

PREFACE

CHAPTER I

EGYPTIAN TWISTED OR PLAITED LACE I

CHAPTER II

MATERIALS 5

Pillows—Cover cloths—Sliders—The pattern—Bobbins—Spangles—Threads
— Bobbin winder — Pins — Pricker or needle-pin — Pricking board — Blue
paper

CHAPTER III

GENERAL METHODS II

To wind bobbins—The slip-knot—Coupling bobbins—To cut off bobbins in
pairs—Broken threads—Weaver's and reef knots—To hang two pairs of
bobbins from a pin—How to handle the bobbins—To make a stitch—Twisting
the bobbins—Enclosing a pin—To pull the threads up into their right position
—How to "put up" pins

CHAPTER IV

STITCHES 19

Whole or cloth stitch—Whole stitch braid with edge—Half-stitch—Reversed
half-stitch—Woven plait, leadwork, or cutwork—Raised plait—Half-stitch
plaits or bars and picots—Half-stitch plaits with single picot—A double
picot—Method of joining a plait or leg to an edge braid—Centre crossing of
six plaits or leadworks—centre crossing of eight plaits or leadworks

CHAPTER V

TORCHON LACE 31

Sizes of threads—Torchon pricking—To repeat prickings by means of parch-
ments—Torchon ground—Torchon edge—Torchon grounds with two or three
twists—Torchon edging No. 1—Torchon edgings Nos. 2 and 3—Torchon
edging No. 3—Torchon insertion sampler—Torchon "twisted half-stitch"
ground—Torchon double ground—Torchon spider—Twisted spider—Plaits
used in Torchon lace—Torchon "rose" grounds or fillings—Rose ground or
Filling, Nos. 1–11

CONTENTS

CHAPTER VI

TORCHON CORNERS 60

Repeating mirror—To work square borders—To finish off a square border —Torchon corners, Nos. 1, 2, 3

CHAPTER VII

EMBROIDERY FINISHINGS 70

Cords—Braids—Edgings—Insertions—Fringes

CHAPTER VIII

CLUNY AND BEDS-MALTESE 76

Cluny lace—Beds-Maltese lace—Cluny edging—Cluny corner—Beds-Maltese edging and corner

CHAPTER IX

HONITON LACE 86

Honiton threads—The small Honiton sampler—Honiton clothing—Honiton braid stitches—Plain hole—Plain hole in curved braid—Mittens—"Four-pin" bud—Five-, six-, seven-, and eight-pin buds—Winkie pins or "snatch pins"— Zigzag holes—Braid dividing into two—Gimp threads—Crossing gimps, 1st, 2nd, and 3rd methods—Curved braids and corners—To work a blind pin—Gaining on a pin—Picots and purl edge—To add and take out bobbins— To tie out—Setting up and getting rid of knots—Sewings—Turning stitch and ten-stick—Ten-stick or stem-stitch—A scroll terminating in a round form—Honiton leaves—raised Honiton lace—Raised leaf divided into little sections called "taps"—Leaf with serrations—Leaf with veins raised on half-stitch—Flower petal—Honiton backgrounds: various methods—Honiton fillings—To work in a filling: various types

CHAPTER X

BUCKS "POINT GROUND" 141

Designing and pattern-making—Table of angles—Sizes of threads—Clothing or heavier parts—Fancy holes and spotted grounds—Pure edge—Gimp threads—Bucks point ground or trolley net—Plaits in net ground—Bucks "honeycomb" net or filling—Whole stitch honeycomb—Kat stitch or wire ground—Point ground fillings—Pin chain—Honeycomb with plaits— Spotted kat stitch—Various types of fillings—Point ground insertions and Edgings (various)—Designing corners

INDEX 182

A MANUAL OF
HAND-MADE BOBBIN LACE WORK

CHAPTER I

EGYPTIAN TWISTED OR PLAITED LACE

THERE seems little doubt that bobbin lace originated from the old Egyptian plaited work, specimens of which were found at Herakleopolis Magna during excavations of 1903–4 and various Egyptian tombs. These fragments show two distinct kinds of work. One kind is of netting (Victoria and Albert Museum, No. 322—1889), in which each crossing of threads is fastened by a knot. Evidently, "Filet" lace originated from this. It is made with a needle and continuous thread. The other kind, illustrated in the front of book (Victoria and Albert Museum, No. 50—1891), consists of twisted threads without knots and seems more likely to be the origin of bobbin made lace. It will be noticed that the

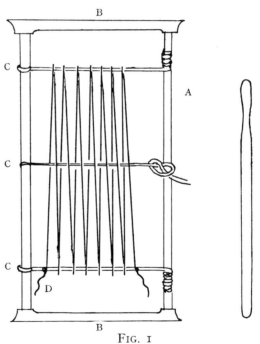

FIG. I

earlier kinds of bobbin lace are made of twisted or plaited threads only. The knots which sometimes occur in bobbin laces are to be found in the more modern and complicated varieties, the knots being used for finishing of threads and not for forming part of the actual

I

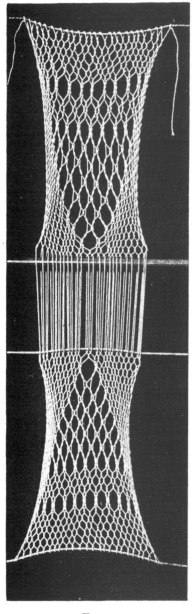

FIG. 2

work. The twisted Egyptian work was made on a frame (Fig. 1). There were 2 vertical rods *A* and *A* which were kept rigid by 2 horizontal bars *B* and *B*. Then 3 cords *C*, *C*, and *C*, were fastened across, one near the top, one near the bottom, and one between. The thread to be plaited was wound upon these 3 cords. One end is tied to the bottom foundation cord at *D* and wound over and under the 3 cords in a manner that allowed the fingers of the worker's left hand to be slipped in between the threads coming from the front and those coming from behind the top foundation cord. The other end of the thread is tied to the bottom foundation cord. By this means the threads were twisted or plaited by using the fingers only, the front threads dropping back and the back threads being pulled forward. This plaiting was worked across in rows in the middle of the work which, of course, twisted the top and bottom simultaneously; upon the completion of each row a stick was inserted and the rows were pushed up and down into position (in accompanying photograph in which the frame does not show); a black stick and a cord are left in to illustrate the method more clearly. When a sufficient length was made, the twisting could be continued by using several threads instead of single threads which shape it to a waist in the middle. It is next removed from the frame, then folded in two, and the unfinished threads are knotted together so as to form a tassel of loops. The sides are joined by a thread being twisted in and out. The work, instead of being joined into a bag as described above, is

FIG. 3

sometimes cut across the middle and the ends are tied (see accompanying photograph). There will then be two pieces. The next step towards bobbin lace was to use several shorter lengths of thread instead of the continuous one (suggested, no doubt, by cutting the threads across), and then the ends of these threads were fastened to bobbins or handles, with which to plait the threads instead of using the fingers only. The next step was to place it on to a cushion or pillow, discarding the wooden frame, and later on pins were used to hold the threads in position. It is easy to follow the progress of the various bobbin plaitings and weavings until they developed into one of the most beautiful arts. Light is thrown on the subject by an engraving in Mrs. Bury Palliser's *History of Lace,* after a picture by Martin de Vos (1581), in which a girl is seen working at the Egyptian plaited work, and at her side another is using a cushion or pillow, and plaiting with weighted threads, but without pins.

CHAPTER II
MATERIALS

Pillows.

THERE are two kinds of pillows necessary for the laces in this book.

1. A round or lobster shape, which revolves as the work proceeds. These pillows are obtainable in several sizes, the smallest of which is let into a well in a larger pillow (or stand) which can be used on a table. These are called French pillows, the little inset pillow revolves. The larger bolster pillows are held on the knees and rest against a table edge, but are much more comfortable when used on pillow stands, called by the midland workers "maids" or "ladies." These bolster shape pillows are used for all Torchon, Cluny, Maltese,[1] Bucks Point, and other laces where the ground and design are worked in conjunction with each other.

2. The mushroom or flat pillow is really a circular piece of wood, padded so as to be highest in the centre, and gradually sloping to the edge. This is used for Honiton, and other sprig laces, in working which it is often necessary to turn the work about, but, whatever the shape, the pillow must be very evenly padded and tightly packed, so that the pins can be inserted easily, and firmly, in order to prevent the lace from being uneven, and curves spoiled.

Cover Cloths.

The pillow should have a movable cover of washable material, of smooth and even texture (linen being the best), so as to allow the pins to enter easily, and also two pieces of the same material (which should be hemmed); one being used to pin over the pattern and finished lace, the other to pin over that part of the pattern on which the bobbins rest. These, besides keeping the work clean, prevent the threads from catching on the pins, pattern, or finished lace. They should be frequently washed. A dull dark green (which must

[1] That is the Maltese variety of lace made in Beds, and other counties of England.

be fast dyed) is restful to the eyes, but some workers prefer white. Instead of the two cover cloths, a square cloth with a circular hole in the middle can be used on a mushroom pillow. A small pincushion is advisable.

Sliders.

These are thin pieces of horn (like those used in very old farm lanterns). They are placed over the parts of Honiton lace where the pins have been pushed down closely. The cover cloths keep the sliders in position, but allow them to slide as required by a touch of the finger. Not only do they help to keep the lace clean, they also prevent the threads from catching on the pins; as they are semi-transparent, the worker is able to see the lace while it is in progress.

Unfortunately, this horn is very difficult to obtain now, but I find a piece of transparent parchment with a circular hole in the middle is perhaps better.

The Pattern.

This consists of a card or parchment, with the pinholes pricked in it, and some markings to guide the worker. Brown glazed board, or saffron-tinted card, can be used, but parchment is necessary when the pattern has to be used many times. The accuracy of the pattern is of the greatest importance. First it is pencilled upon drawing paper (the sectional variety being very helpful for geometrical laces), then the various stitches are carefully chosen, and noted by drawing or special lace-making signs. Then the drawing is placed over a piece of pricking card, or under a piece of transparent parchment, and both are pinned on to a pillow or pricking board; the pinholes are next pricked through with a needle pin of the same thickness as the lace pins. The necessary markings are now put in on the card, or parchment. The working drawing should be kept by the student and used for reference.

It is far more interesting for the worker to make her own designs, and this is not nearly such a difficult task as is generally supposed.

Bobbins.

Three kinds of bobbins are illustrated.

1. The Torchon bobbin is rather large, and therefore suitable for the coarser laces; its long spool takes length of thread which is

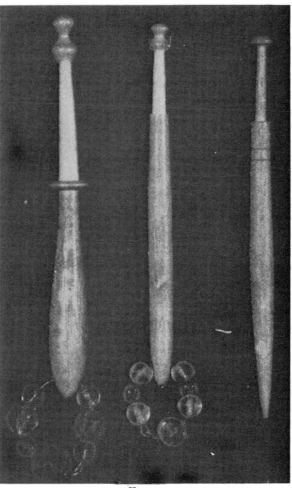

FIG. 4

required to prevent frequently knotting. The little "neck" at the top, used for the slip-knot, enables the weighted bobbin to hang in such a way as is more convenient to the worker.

2. The Bucks bobbin is smaller and the shank is all down alike on account of the large number of bobbins often used. The spool is large enough to hold the long length of fine thread.

3. The Honiton bobbin is not required to carry so much thread, and, as it is never weighted, the slip-knot is made on to the wound thread. The other end tapers for the purpose of taking "sewings."

Gimp Bobbins.

These are larger bobbins of the same shape, sometimes used for the outlining threads of either the Bucks or Honiton laces.

Spangles.

The Torchon and Bucks bobbins are provided with a hole, through which a wire ring of beads or "spangles"[1] is hung. This serves two purposes: (1) their weight helps to keep the threads in position; (2) the ring prevents the thread from twisting or from becoming entangled with others.

When a large number of bobbins is used, they can (if weighted) be moved more easily from one part of the pillow to another and still retain their places, which would be impossible without beaded bobbins. It is a great hindrance and annoyance to beginners to be continually untangling their threads.

Threads.

Linen, cotton, silk, wool, and metal are all suitable for lace-making.

The cotton, a gassed thread, is used for Honiton, and much of the Maltese and Bucks Points. It is called skip or slip thread. Linen thread is used for Torchon, Cluny, Maltese, and Bucks Point.

A shiny linen thread, called "gimp," is used for outlining both Honiton and Bucks Point.

Silk, wool, and metal are suitable for making cords, braids, insertions, narrow edgings, and fringes.

Threads should be kept in blue paper in order to retain their whiteness. Do not handle threads more than absolutely necessary.

[1] It is better to use this word rather than "jingles." Gimp bobbins surrounded by loose rings are called "jingles."

MATERIALS

Bobbin Winder.

A turn or winder saves much time, those made of metal being much more durable than the wooden ones, which quickly wear out. If the thread is in skeins, a skein holder is necessary, but an ordinary "wool winder" will do.

Pins.

For lace-making there are special pins, which are of better quality, finer, and longer, than ordinary pins.

Avoid using fancy pins, which are often uneven and quickly rust.

The sizes most suitable for the different laces are—

LL—for the finest Honiton.
LLL—for coarser Honiton.
LW—for Bucks "point ground."
DLW—for Torchon and Beds-Maltese.

Laundry pins (a much heavier make) are used for Cluny.

Pricker or Needle-pin.

This can be made by driving a needle firmly into a wooden handle. It is used for making prickings and "taking up sewings."

Pricking Board.

A cork mat, with flannel or felt fastened to it, is useful for making prickings. Its advantages over the lace pillow are: (1) it is quite flat; (2) the pricker always enters to the same depth, and therefore makes the holes of uniform size.

The design and card or parchment are kept in position with drawing pins.

PRICKING CARD. This is a very strong, shiny, brown card, called glazed board. It is suitable for most prickings.

PARCHMENT. This is essential when much work has to be made from one pricking. It should be as transparent as possible to facilitate making the pricking.

BLUE PAPER. In order to keep finished lace a good colour, blue tissue-paper is best for wrapping. A thicker, smooth, dark blue paper is necessary where strength is required.

All materials for lace-making can be obtained from the author, at 23 Links Road, London, S.W.17.

CHAPTER III
GENERAL METHODS

To Wind Bobbins.

HOLD the bobbin horizontally in the right hand, or place it in the nozzle of a winder, twist the thread a few times round the bobbin over and towards you, then turn the bobbin in the reverse direction, winding evenly and tightly. When you have finished, a slip-knot prevents it from coming undone, and at the same time (by turning the bobbin to the left) allows the thread to unwind slowly when required.

The Slip-knot.

If the bobbin is spangled, hold it horizontally in the left hand, also holding the loose end of the thread. Take the thread in the right hand so that the finger and thumb hold that part of the thread farthest from the bobbin, then twist it round the little neck, over and under towards you, three times (or more if the thread is of silk). The loose thread can now be pulled up tightly, care being taken that it does not slip either lower down or off the end of the bobbin (Fig. 5, *left*).

For a Honiton bobbin, hold it horizontally in the right hand, also holding the loose end of the thread, put your left-hand fingers under the thread, twist it right over towards you, forming a loop, and having placed the bobbin head through the loop, pull tightly (Fig. 5, *right*).

Coupling Bobbins.

In Torchon and similar laces, the bobbins are often tied together in bunches and hung upon a pin, the ends of the thread being trimmed off afterwards.

This method saves time but is very untidy, and, indeed, is impossible when the lace has to be neatly joined as for borders, etc. It is never permissible in the better laces, so when winding, the

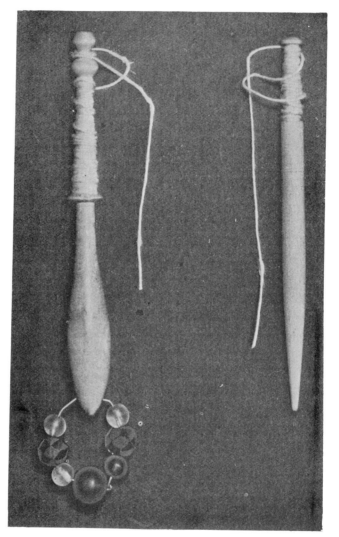

FIG. 5

bobbins must be coupled by over-winding one, and then winding part of this thread on to another bobbin, leaving the bobbins a few inches apart. They are hung from one of the pins forming the pattern.

To Cut off Bobbins in Pairs.

Hold the pair of bobbins together in the left hand, take a pair of scissors (with the screw slightly loosened) in the right hand, put the

12

closed scissors under the threads, and twist the scissors right over towards you, down, and away from you. This forms a loop, through which take hold of the threads with the points of the scissors, taking care not to cut them until after the thread is pulled through, and the knot drawn tightly; then pull the bobbins, which should slip away from the cut threads, and the bobbins will be found knotted together.

Broken Threads.

A break sometimes necessitates undoing a small piece of lace, until the end is long enough to tie; if it is a passive thread, it can often be hung in its place from a pin, and then woven in with the others, the ends being cut off afterwards. If it is a leader the broken ends can be knotted with a weaver's knot, and arranged when at the end of a row to change places with a passive, the knot being cut away later.

KNOTS

Weaver's Knot.

ITS USES. This is used for joining broken threads, or adding new ones should there not be sufficient on the bobbin.

HOW TO MAKE IT. Place the two threads to be joined between the finger and thumb of the left hand, leaving short ends of about half an inch free, so that they cross at right angles, the horizontal thread being in front of the other. Take the long thread hanging on the right, twist it over in front of the thumb, round the back of the little vertical end, and in front of the other, thus forming a loop. This loop is also held in place by the thumb and first finger of the left hand while the little horizontal end is being folded over and passed through the loop; the thumb slides back a little and holds it, while the long end is pulled tightly (Fig. 6).

Reef Knot.

ITS USE. This knot is used when "tying out" at the end of a finished part.

HOW TO MAKE IT. Reverse the position of the two bobbins to be tied, so that you use the tail ends. Pass the right-hand bobbin under and over the left, letting it drop through the loop thus formed, and pull up tightly. Then take the bobbins as before, but reverse the movement, pass the right-hand bobbin over and under the other,

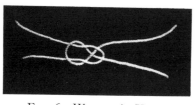

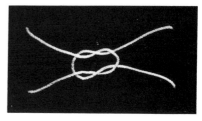

FIG. 6. WEAVER'S KNOT   FIG. 7. REEF KNOT

through the loop, and pull up tightly. It is often advisable to make another knot, again reversing the movement; then cut off (Fig. 7).

To Hang Two Pairs of Bobbins from a Pin.

The bobbins must be coupled without knots (Fig. 8).

Put up the pin and hang one pair round it, hang the other pair round the same pin so that the middle threads cross (right over left), then take the second and fourth threads, pass them over the first and

FIG. 8. TO HANG TWO PAIRS FROM ONE PIN

third threads, and enclose the pin by crossing the two middle threads (2 over 3). This forms a whole stitch round the pin. This method is very useful for commencing Torchon laces, also for adding bobbins while work is in progress, the new pair being hung on to the pin placed in the edge hole of a braid. The leaders are woven through them, the pin is now removed and replaced between the two pairs so that the leaders twist and pass round it to work the next row.

How to Handle the Bobbins.

I am keeping to the usual method of numbering the bobbins from left to right. This applies to the position and not to the actual bobbin; therefore, when 2 bobbins cross each other 1 becomes 2 and 2 becomes 1. This may seem confusing, but is really quite simple in working.

GENERAL METHODS

To Make a Stitch.

A stitch is made with 4 bobbins (2 pairs), one pair being handled with each hand.

To make a whole stitch, lift 2 with the thumb and finger of left hand and place it over 3. Now, using both hands, lift 2 and 4 simultaneously and place them over 1 and 3 respectively, then lift 2 over 3 with left hand.

This is the same in all lace, but when working the lighter kinds (those made without beaded bobbins) the bobbins are lifted as little as possible, almost rolled one over the other. When heavier laces are worked, the bobbins are lifted from the pillow and dropped down into their new places, their weight helping them to fall in the right position.

Twisting the Bobbins.

Always twist the bobbins to the left.

Enclosing a Pin.

Enclosing or "covering" a pin means either completing a stitch that is partly made, the pin being "put up" in the middle of it; or working another stitch so that the pin is surrounded by threads.

To Pull the Threads up into their Right Position.

At frequent intervals (sometimes after each stitch) the threads must be pulled up more or less tightly into place, according to the kind of lace, size of thread, etc. The thicker the thread, the more it wants pulling. When using weighted bobbins they will naturally fall between the fingers, so that they can be pulled up independently, one rather more tightly than the other, should it be necessary. When using Honiton bobbins, the leaders are held together in the hand, the thumb controlling the pressure on both, so that they also can be regulated one more tightly than the other. The passives of Honiton lace are not often required to be pulled tightly, but by passing the back of the fingers of the hand across them they can be rolled into position.

Whenever bobbins are pulled up into position, always pull them in the direction in which they are travelling in the lace.

The bobbins should hang evenly, all having about the same length of thread between the bobbin and the lace. The worker should get into the habit of slightly turning a bobbin to the left and lengthening the thread whenever it becomes shorter than the others. The length of thread required free should be about the same length as the bobbin.

The bobbins must serve as handles for the threads. Never handle the thread with the fingers.

How to " Put up " Pins.

The use of the pins is to hold a thread or threads in position until the lace is sufficiently advanced to be able to retain its shape.

Those pins whose duty is to hold the outline or edges of the lace in position should be inserted in the pillow so that they slant a little, just sufficient for the lace threads to pull against them, otherwise the strain put upon the pins while continuing the work will pull them over and the outline be lost, in which case the worker will see her lace gradually rising from the pattern instead of remaining flat upon it.

The pins in groundings and inner parts of lace should be vertical or inclined if anything to lean slightly back, but all pins should stand up about the same height.

These remarks will perhaps appear trivial, but necessarily the pillow of a good worker always presents a tidy appearance.

Bobbin lace stitches are made up of two movements of the bobbins—

> Left over right is called "Cross."
> Right over left is called "Turn."

The stitches are easily explained and quickly written by abbreviating the words to their initial letter.

Movements	Abbreviations	Stitches
Cross, Turn	C.T.	Half-stitch
Cross, Turn, Cross	C.T.C.	Whole stitch
Thus,	P. means Pin.	

Cross.	Turn.	Pin.	Cross.	Turn.	
C.	T.	P.	C.	T.	Denotes the Torchon grounding.

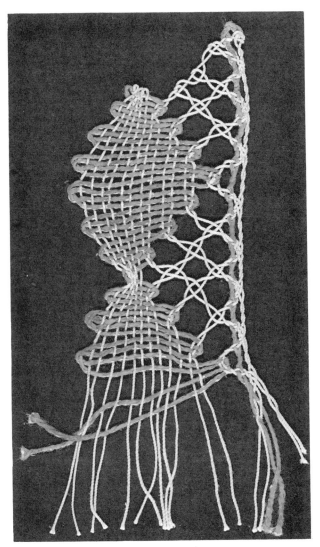

FIG. 9

It is better to use the word "twist" instead of "turn" when the bobbins repeat the movement more than once.

I have not used this method through the book, as it may be confusing to those who have some knowledge of lace-making, but it is certainly quicker and better for those who have not handled bobbins before.

There are various kinds of coloured diagrams which simplify lace-making.

Fig. 9 shows one of my own methods in which the colours show the direction the different threads travel.

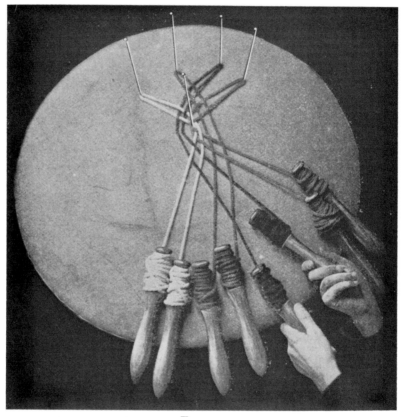

FIG. 10

The coloured diagram method used at the Normal Lace School of Bruges indicates the numbers of threads used.

A demonstration pillow with large bobbins and thick coloured cords is useful for teaching various stitches to classes. (See Fig. 10.)

CHAPTER IV
STITCHES

Whole or Cloth Stitch (Fig. 11).

THIS stitch is made with two pairs of bobbins.

Counting the four threads from left to right, pass the second over third, second over first, and fourth over third. These two should move simultaneously, using both hands Then pass the second over the third again.

THE PRICKING Place a piece of sectional paper over a piece of pricking card, pin both to a pillow or pricking board, then with a needle-pin make two vertical rows of holes about five divisions of the paper apart. The holes must be pricked at every other point where the lines of the paper cross, and the holes of the second row must alternate with those of the first row. At the top prick holes B, C, D, and E (Fig. 12). Remove the sectional paper, and pin the pricked card firmly to the lace pillow.

TO WORK THE BRAID. Hang a pair of bobbins on a pin at A, also four pairs from B, C, D, and E. The pair from A is called the "leader pair," or "workers," because they travel across the braid from side to side, weaving over and under the others, which remain stationary and are for this reason called "passives."

With the first two pairs, make a whole stitch (2 over 3, 2 and 4 over 1 and 3, 2 over 3), put the left-hand pair aside and work the leaders in whole stitch through the next pair of passives in the same way, continuing until the leaders have woven through all the passives. Twist the leaders twice to the left and holding them in right hand, pull up into place, put a pin in hole 1 under the leaders so that they pass round this pin ready to make the next row. The stitches are made exactly as before. Do not attempt to reverse the whole stitch movement, or an uneven braid will result. For the next row, work leaders through all the passives in whole stitch, twist leaders twice, pull up into position with left hand, put a pin in hole 2, bring leaders round it for next row. It will be found necessary to keep the passives pulled down tightly into their places as the work proceeds, but never handle the threads with the fingers. Use the lower part of the bobbin as a handle for the thread.

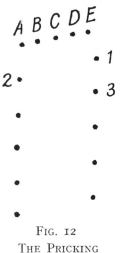

FIG. II. THE STITCH

Whole Stitch Braid with Edge (*Fig. 25, right side*).

Pricking as before. Hang two pairs of bobbins on a pin at *A*. The first pair

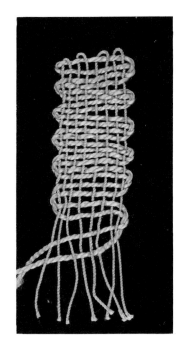

FIG. 12
THE PRICKING

FIG. 13. BRAID

is the edge pair and should be twisted three times; the second pair, also twisted three times, is the leader pair. Hang three pairs of passives upon the three centre pins, *B*, *C*, and *D*, and one edge pair at hole *E*. Bring leaders from the left through the three passives in whole stitch; twist leaders three times, work them in whole stitch with the right

20

FIG. 14. THE STITCH

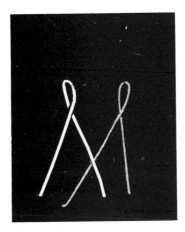

FIG. 15. REVERSED HALF-STITCH

hand edge pair, and twist both pairs three times; put up a pin in hole 1 so that they pass behind it. Twist each pair three times. The leaders and edge pair have now changed places, leave the outside pair and work leaders back through the three pairs of passives in whole stitch, twist leaders three times, put up pin so that they pass behind it, work whole stitch with edge pair, twist each three times, working back again with the second pair.

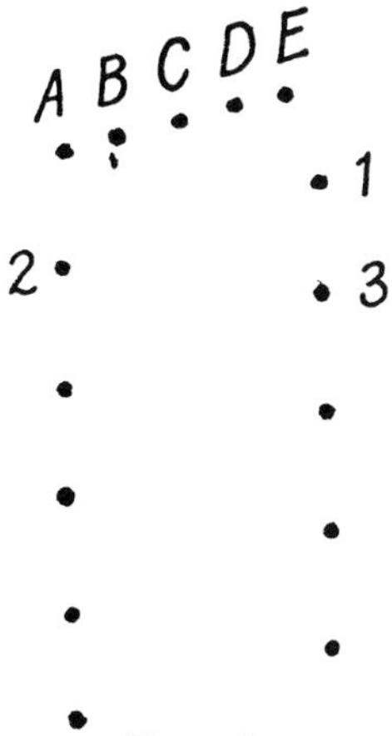

Half-stitch (Fig. 14).

This stitch is made with two pairs of bobbins. Counting the four threads from left to right, pass the second one over the third, then pass the second over first, and fourth over third; these two should move simultaneously, using both hands.

FIG. 16.
THE PRICKING

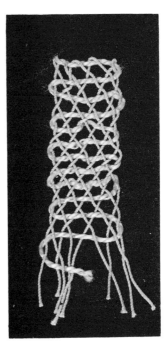

FIG. 17.
HALF-STITCH BRAID

21

THE PRICKING is made as for the whole stitch braid.

TO MAKE THE BRAID. Hang a pair of "leaders" at *A* and four pairs of passives for the centre of braid, twist each pair once to the left; commence on the left side, making a half stitch (2 over 3, 2 over 1, and 4 over 3), leave the two left-hand pairs, use the right-hand pair and the next pair on right to make the next half stitch, repeating to end of row. It will be noticed that only one "leader" thread runs across the braid, and that each pair of bobbins is left twisted once to the left. When at the end of row, give the leader

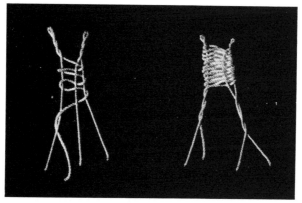

FIG. 18

pair one extra twist in order to bring it in position for the next row, pull up into position, put up a pin in hole 1 under the leaders and bring them round to work the next row.

Reversed Half-stitch (Fig. 15).

This is exactly the reverse of a half-stitch.

It is only used for closing fancy holes. (See Fig. 101.)

THE STITCH. With four threads, counting from left to right. Pass the second and fourth over the first and third. Then the second over the third.

Woven Plait, Leadwork or Cutwork.

This pretty little stitch is to be found in nearly all pillow-made laces. It consists of three foundation threads, upon which another thread is woven closely. Figs. 18 and 19 show three different shapes

22

as well as the method of working. The name varies according to the lace in which it is made. Honiton workers call it "Leadwork" or "Cutwork" while the other lace makers call it a plait or "Tally."

Two pairs of bobbins without knots are required, three of which hang down as passives, while the other weaves or darns over and under the 3 passives. The weaver is held loosely. It changes from one hand to the other as required, but must not be allowed to drop or it will draw up the work. The passives are lifted and dropped again as the weaver passes under them.

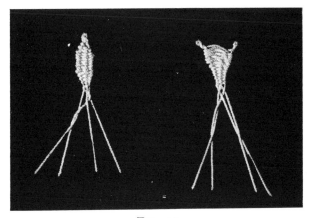

FIG. 19

To WEAVE THE PLAIT. Commence with the second thread as leader (it must be longer than the others), pass it over 3, under and over 4, under 2, over and under 1. The stitch must now be pulled up. Keeping the leader between the thumb and first finger of the left hand, take the first bobbin between the second and third fingers of the same hand. Take the other two bobbins between the thumb and finger, and second and third fingers, of right hand in a similar way. Pull the leader a little *very* gently. (This movement controls the width of the plait.) Holding the centre passive firmly in the direction in which the plait is being worked, pull or spread the two outside passives more widely apart (this pushes the woven thread up closely). Continue plaiting and pulling up until sufficient length is woven.

Beginners must pull up at every row, but with practice it is not necessary to pull up so often.

Raised Plait (*Fig. 20*).

Used in Beds-Maltese, Cluny lace, and occasionally Torchon. It is a plait made upon a ground of clothwork or half-stitch. When the whole stitch ground is woven up to where the plait is to be,

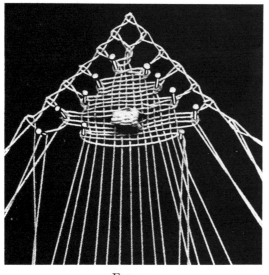

FIG. 20

work the leaders to edge, put up pin, enclose, and leave. Make a long plait with the two middle pairs, leave this, and bring the leaders through again, taking in those which made the plait. Care must be taken to close up the whole stitch ground as much as possible. In order to raise the plait into position, a little stick or roll of paper can be used, but with a little practice it is not necessary.

Sometimes these plaits are allowed to lie quite flat and are then made in leaf shape with a whole stitch at both ends. These are made in the usual way, but a few rows of the groundwork are woven before taking in the threads from the plait. For this style of raised plaiting more ground passives are better.

Half-stitch Plaits or Bars and Picots (*Figs. 21–23*).

These half-stitch, or plaited, bars, called by the Midland lace-makers "legs" or "straps," are used to connect the different parts of the lace and also for the edges. They are made with or without the addition of "Picots."

PICOTS. Purl pins, or turn pins. The picot is a tiny loop used

24

to finish the outer edges of many laces, they are also used on one or both sides of plaited bars and are sometimes found in fillings (Figs. 22 and 23).

Some workers are now making picots on the head side of Torchon lace. The reason is that as the picot is one of the stitches that up to now cannot be exactly reproduced by machine, it is introduced to mark it as "hand made." This practice is not advisable as the picot is not a suitable stitch for this type of lace. The better method would be a slight change in suitable places of the usual stitches.

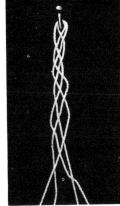

To Work the Plait. Use two pairs of bobbins, and make a succession of half-stitches as shown in the diagram. Of course, these should be evenly and rather tightly worked, so that the plait will lie flat like a tiny braid.

Six-thread Plait. Occasionally, six threads are used to make a plait, but only when six are required for the working of other parts.

FIG. 21

To work it, weave the third pair through two pairs in whole stitch, and then the third pair again through two pairs, and so on.

Half-stitch Plaits with Single Picot (*Fig. 23, left side*).

Single picots or loops are used for Cluny and Beds-Maltese laces in which the double twist would look too clumsy.

To Make the Single Picot (Fig. 22). (On the left-hand side of a bar.) Make a plait to where a pinhole denotes a picot, hold the outside thread in the left hand and a pin in the right, make a loop by twisting the thread round the pin (over and under towards you),

FIG. 22

and put up the pin in the pinhole, then pull into position. Twist the next thread over the end one and continue the plait, taking care not to drag the picot open. It should remain the size of the pin it encloses.

When making a picot on the right edge of a bar in order to obtain the same twist (in both cases the bobbin end of the thread should come from *under* the other), the loop must be made by twisting the outside thread round the pin *under and over*, then twist the end thread over the next thread (Fig. 23, left side).

WINDMILL. The crossing of two half-stitch plaits is called a "windmill." With the four pairs of bobbins hanging from the two

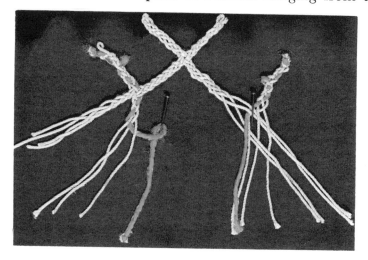

FIG. 23

plaits to be crossed, use the bobbins in pairs instead of singly. Make a half-stitch, put up a pin in the hole between the pairs, enclose it with one twist which completes a whole stitch with the pin in the middle, then proceed with making the two plaits to the next two pin-holes, of course using the bobbins singly again (Fig. 23, right side).

A Double Picot (Fig. 24).

The double picot should be used for all fine work.

It is made with the leader pair after passing through the "edge" or end pair. Twist the leaders five to seven times according to the size of the thread, make a twist (or loop like the single picot), then as you are pulling up the thread, twist the second thread also round the pin in the same direction, so that the two threads twist together as they pass round the pin. Let the last thread fall as the outside

26

thread, and twist the next one over it, so that the first thread to twist round the pin will be the outside thread when finished. Pass the picot pair back into the lace as leaders and continue the work. The diagram shows the picot left open. It consists of a loop of twisted threads which joins by one thread passing under and the other thread over the twisted part before the final twist is given. Badly made picots "split" or untwist after the pin is removed, but a little care will prevent this.

Method of Joining a Plait or Leg to an Edge Braid (Fig. 25).

This method, although not much used in this country, has the advantages of being simple, neater, and stronger than the usual way

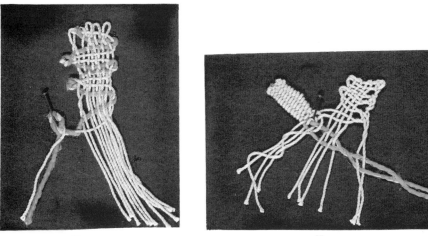

FIG. 24   FIG. 25

of joining plaits, or legs, to the braid, by weaving the leaders of the braid through the two pairs to be joined, then twisting the leaders, passing them round a pin, and weaving them back again.

For joining a plait to the braid on the left-hand side. Finish weaving so that the leader thread is the third from the left, and leave.

To MAKE THE JOIN. Weave the braid leaders through both the pairs from the plait. Put up a pin between these two pairs and enclose the pin with a whole stitch. Use the pair coming through from the plait as leaders and continue the braid. The old leader

27

pair from the braid is now used with the other pair from the plait, to weave the next plait. For this plait, use the third thread from the left as the leader, passing it over and under the end thread. By this means, the same leader is used for both plaits, and prevents the first plait from being drawn up out of shape. Legs are joined into a braid in exactly the same way.

Centre Crossing of Six Plaits or Leadworks (Figs. 26 and 27).

This method of crossing should result in a centre hole. It is also used in Cluny lace, and occasionally in Honiton.

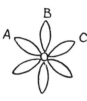

FIG. 26

TO WORK IT. The three upper plaits from *A*, *B*, and *C* having been finished, work a whole stitch to draw up each one. Then use each pair of bobbins together as one thread, but do not get them twisted.

Pass the left pair of the centre pairs under the next pair to the left.

Pass the right pair of the centre pairs over the next pair to the right.

Cross the two centre pairs, right over left.

Pass the left pair of the centre pairs out to the left under and over the next two pairs.

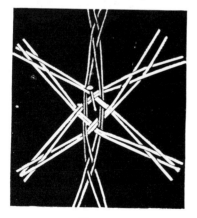

FIG. 27

Pass the right pair of the centre pairs out to the right over and under the next two pairs.

A pin may be placed in the centre to keep all steady.

Pass the left pair of the centre pairs under the next pair to the left.

Pass the right pair of the centre pairs over the next pair to the right.

Cross the two centre pairs right over left.

Pass the left pair of the centre pairs under the next pair to the left.

Pass the right pair of the centre pairs over the next pair to the right.

28

Pull up carefully into position.

Use the bobbins again singly. Make a whole stitch with each set of 4, and then make the three lower plaits of leadworks.

Centre Crossing of Eight Plaits or Leadworks (Figs. 28 and 29).

This method of crossing, which should result in a centre hole, is used in Cluny and Torchon lace. (See Torchon Sampler, Fig. 31.)

To WORK IT. The four upper plaits from *A*, *B*, *C*, and *D* having been worked, make a whole stitch to draw up each one. Then use each pair of bobbins together as one thread, but do not let them get twisted.

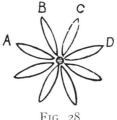

FIG. 28

Make a half-stitch with the centre four pairs.

Make a half-stitch with the right-hand four pairs.

Make a half-stitch with the left-hand four pairs.

Repeat these three half-stitches.

A pin may be put up in the centre to keep all steady.

Make a whole stitch with the centre four pairs.

Of the right-hand four pairs, cross the centre two left over right.

Of the left-hand four pairs, cross the centre two left over right.

Pull up carefully into position.

Use the bobbins again singly, make a whole stitch with each set of 4, and then make the four lower plaits or leadworks.

FIG. 29

THE SAMPLERS

In designing and working the samplers in this book, I have endeavoured to show the greatest variety of stitches and methods in a limited space, also to give an idea of the relative size and general appearance of the finished fillings, so that the student can tell at a glance which is most suitable for her purpose. The stitches are also worked out separately, each being accompanied by enlarged prickings, and working diagrams, as well as description.

The diagrams must not be taken as examples of finished work, but as a means to convey the method of working to the student. For this reason, many of them are left too open, so as to illustrate the stitch better, also the threads are necessarily out of proportion.

A red thread is sometimes used to make the illustration plainer.*

There are many fillings, which space will not permit me to reproduce. The most important ones and their varieties are fully described. After working these the student should have no difficulty in copying others from old specimens of lace.

* In this edition illustrated either by a shaded grey or solid white.

CHAPTER V
TORCHON LACE

TORCHON lace, which is of continental origin, is now made in this country. Owing to its durability it is suitable for many domestic purposes. For the student who requires a good all round knowledge, it is the best to commence with.

First read through the notes on the general methods which apply to all lace; then make the pricking, and work out the Torchon ground and edge (page 37).

Next prick and work the first edging, and perhaps one or both of the others. After this it is advisable to make a strip of edging, or insertion to practice upon, and to keep as a sampler for reference. It should contain spaces for fillings, groundings, and spottings, as well as cloth and half-stitch work.

The pricking and insertion given on page 44 are intended to show what is suitable for a sampler. The worker should arrange and draw out her own if possible.

Sizes of Threads.

I am giving a few sizes of threads with the proportionate size of the sectional paper to be used for the pricking.

Although these will be found satisfactory for most Torchon laces, the worker must use her own discretion.

Some persons work more tightly than others, and some few patterns will require a coarser or finer thread.

A very good size for beginners to use is No. 50,[1] and the pricking should be made on 10 to the inch paper.

Torchon Pricking.

TO MAKE THE PRICKING FOR EDGING No. 1 (Fig. 38). Take a strip of squared paper, and with a pencil make a row of six dots

---

[1] The thread referred to is of the best quality, specially made for lace-making.

HAND-MADE BOBBIN LACE WORK

TORCHON SAMPLER STITCHES

Sampler space · (Figs. 30 and 31) · Described on page

1. Torchon edge 37
2. Torchon ground with 1 twist between pins 37
3. Torchon ground with 2 twists between pins 38
4. Torchon ground with 3 twists between pins 38
5. Twisted half-stitch ground with 1 twist between pins . . . 45
7. Twisted half-stitch ground with 2 twists between pins . . . 46
6. Twisted half-stitch ground with 3 twists between pins . . . 46
8. Torchon double ground 46
8. Whole or cloth trail 44
   Half-stitch trail 45
11. ⎫
12. ⎬ Spotted Torchon grounds with plaits differently arranged . . 47
13. ⎪
14. ⎭
17. Spider 46
17. Spider and twisted spider 47
15. ⎫ Plaits crossed 28
16. ⎭
25. Rose ground or filling, No. 1 49
26. Rose ground or filling, No. 2 50
18. Rose ground or filling, No. 3. Also see sampler insertion middle space. 51
20. Rose ground or filling, No. 5 53
23. Closed check ground or filling, No. 6 54
19. Closed check ground or filling, No. 7 56
29. Torchon ground or filling, No. 9 58
21. Torchon ground or filling, No. 8 57
22. Torchon ground or filling, No. 8. See top middle space of sampler
    insertion 44
24. Torchon ground or filling, No. 11 59
27. Diamonds of whole stitch 43
28. Small diamonds of half-stitch 43
    Torchon ground or filling, No. 10. See sampler insertion lowest middle
    space 44

Sectional Paper						Size of lace thread	
6 to the inch	.	.	.	.	.	No.	18
8 ,, ,,	.	.	.	.	.	,,	25–35
10 ,, ,,	.	.	.	.	.	,,	35–60
12 ,, ,,	.	.	.	.	.	,,	50–100
14 ,, ,,	.	.	.	.	.	,,	70–100
16 ,, ,,	.	.	.	.	.	,,	90–120

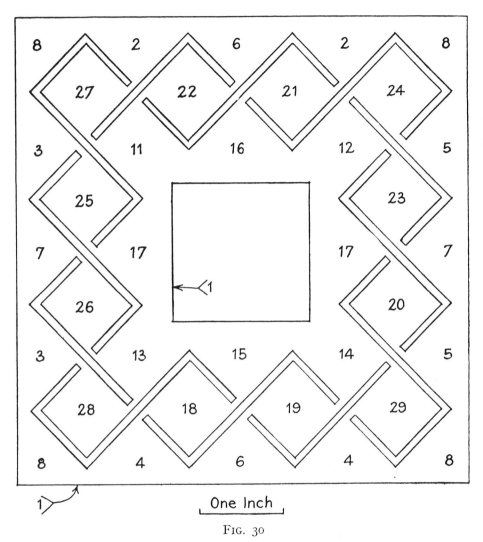

FIG. 30

along a line and at every other point where the other lines cross it
(Fig. 32). Then make a second row of five dots on the next line above
it; they should alternate with those of the first row. Above this
make a similar row of four dots, then one of three dots, then one of
two, and at the top put one dot.

Now make another little triangle of dots, allowing the last three
of the first triangle to form the first three of the next, and repeat

33

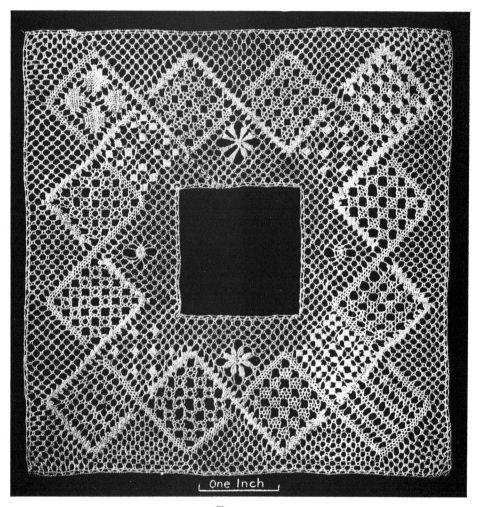

One Inch

FIG. 31

this several times. Next, draw the curved outline from the top of one triangle to the top of the next. These curves must be quite alike and can be repeated by means of tracing-paper if necessary. Upon this curved outline mark dots, at points where the edge pins are to be, in order to get the right number of holes and to space them correctly, pencil lightly the pathway taken by the "leaders" when travelling to and fro. The first diagram will explain exactly how the pattern is dotted out. Now place the drawing over a piece of

34

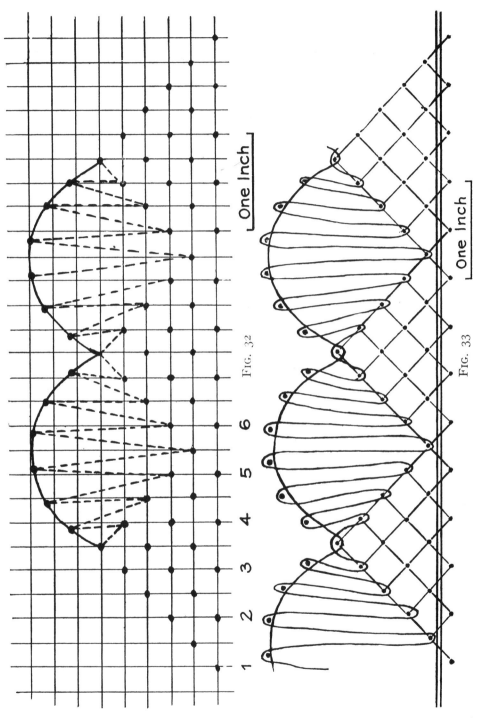

One Inch

Fig. 32

1 2 3 4 5 6

One Inch

Fig. 33

pricking card, or under a piece of transparent parchment, and pin both firmly to a pillow or pricking-board. Take a needle-pin of the same size as the lace pins to be used, hold it vertically and prick through both drawing and card or parchment, at every dot.

Remove the drawing, and with a fine pen, and Indian ink, put in the markings, showing the edge (called "foot side"), direction of the groundwork, the outline of the fan-shaped heads, and the direction the leaders are to work. The second diagram (Fig. 33) shows this marking.

To Repeat Prickings by Means of Parchments.

This method often saves time, and also ensures the "heads" or repeats being quite alike. Draw correctly one repeat, and two extra holes, one on the edge and the other on the "foot side." Make a pricking of it through a transparent piece of parchment. On this parchment scratch a line, right across, through the "foot side" holes, using a needle and a ruler, also put in with ink all necessary markings. Now take a strip of card on which a line is scratched from end to end for the "foot" holes. Pin the card on to the pricking-board, upon it place the little parchment pricking (taking great care that the scratched lines are exactly one over the other), pin both securely down and prick through the holes in the parchment. When one repeat is finished, move the parchment farther along, so that the two extra holes come exactly over the end holes of your first repeat and the "foot side" lines correspond; again pin both down and prick the next repeat, continuing until the length is finished. If a considerable length of lace is required, make the pricking long enough to fit right round the pillow. This saves continually "setting up." ("Setting Up" is described on page 61.)

For pricking a parchment the repeating pattern is placed under the long strip and the holes are pricked through in the same way, the advantage of this being that the markings can be traced on to each "head" as it is pricked. Of course, these little parchment patterns can be used again and again for many years, thus saving time and unnecessary redrawing when copies of the pattern are required.

36

Torchon Ground (*Figs.* 34 *and* 35).

Illustrated in the Torchon sampler, Fig. 30, at 5.

It is pricked and worked diagonally (Fig. 34), two pairs of bobbins being required for each pin-hole. The stitch consists of a half-stitch, a pin being put up between the pairs, and enclosed with a half-stitch.

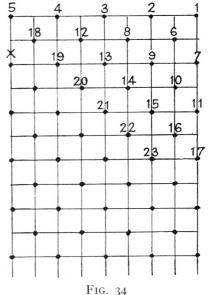

FIG. 34

To Work the Diagram. Wind 12 pairs of bobbins in pairs, as described on page 11, and hang three pairs at the end holes 1 and 5. Hang two pairs at each of the intervening holes, 2, 3, and 4.

Twist the two end pairs three times each, and twist the pair next to each of these twice. Twist the other eight pairs once. With right-hand pair from 2 and left-hand pair from 1, make a half-stitch (2 over 3, 2 over 1, and 4 over 3), put up a pin in hole 6 between the pairs, then enclose it by making another half-stitch, which leaves each pair twisted once. Now make the Torchon edge as under.

Torchon Edge (*Figs.* 34 *and* 35).

Illustrated in Torchon sampler, Fig. 30, at 1. Three pairs of bobbins are needed to work this stitch.

Hole 6 having been enclosed, bring the third pair from the outside through the next pair in whole stitch, twist right-hand pair once and left-hand pair twice, put up pin in hole 7, between them, but do not enclose. With the two edge pairs make a whole stitch, twist outside pair three times and next pair once, then enclose pin 7 by a whole stitch made with the pairs on each side of it. Twist the right-hand pair twice and the left-hand pair once or more as required by the ground. Now continue the Torchon ground. With the right-hand pair from 3 and the left-hand pair from 2, make a half-stitch, pin in hole 8, enclose it with half-stitch, drop the left-hand pair, and take up the pair from hole 6, to use for hole 9. Work the other holes in the same way, and at the end make the edge stitch. Continue

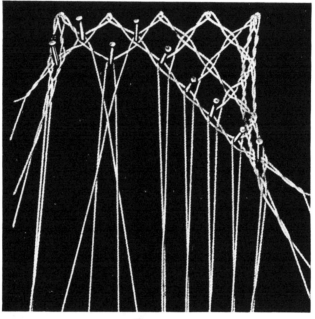

FIG. 35

the rows in succession until hole 25 is complete. The pair from hole 18 is used to make another edge stitch (on the left side of the work) at X which is just the reverse of the edge stitch explained above.

Torchon Grounds with Two or Three Twists.

Illustrated in the Torchon sampler, Fig. 30, at 2 and 3. These are pricked and worked as ordinary Torchon ground, but with one or two extra twists between the pins.

Torchon Edging No. 1 (Figs. 36–38).

After making the pricking (Fig. 36), upon 10 to the inch paper, pin it firmly to the pillow, also pinning on two cover-cloths so that they cover the top and lower part of the pattern, leaving the two top repeats visible.

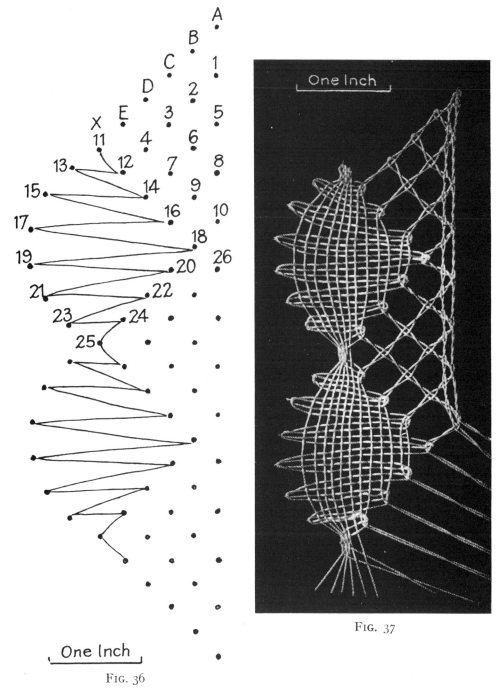

One Inch

FIG. 36

FIG. 37

One Inch

Fig. 38

40

Wind and couple 10 pairs of bobbins, with No. 50 thread.

To Work the Edging. Hang three pairs round a pin in hole *A*, and a pair from each pin in holes *B*, *C*, *D*, and *E*, also four pairs from a pin at *X* just above hole 11. (When one or two rows have been worked, the pins round which the threads were hung can be removed and the bobbins gently pulled down into their places.)

With the six pairs on the right side, work the little triangular-shaped piece of Torchon ground and edge holes 1–10 (described on page 37). There will be one pair hanging from each pin 4, 7, 9, and 10, and these pairs are left ready to be used for the whole stitch fan. With the fourth pair from the left as leaders, work whole stitch out to the edge through three pairs, twist leaders twice, put up a pin in hole 11, under the leaders and next to the end passives, bring the leaders back in whole stitch through the three passives and the twisted pair from hole 4, twist leaders once, put up a pin in hole 12 between them and the end passive pair, work leaders out to edge (always using whole stitch), twist twice, put up pin in hole 13, bring leaders back to 14, take in the pair from hole 7, work out to edge again, and continue until pin 18 is put up and enclosed. The end pair of passives from 18, which have just been taken in from 10, will now drop out again; twist them once and leave for the ground, continue weaving the whole stitch fan in this way, leaving out a pair from each hole on lower inner edge of fan 20, 22, and 24, for the ground.

After hole 25 has been enclosed, the leaders must work back and be left as fourth pair from the end.

Now work the next triangular piece of ground (10 holes) from No. 26, taking in the four pairs from the whole stitch fan, and leaving out the four pairs as before, ready for the next fan. For the succeeding fan use the same leaders left from last fan, which will be found ready to take in the first pair from the ground.

The edging is continued by exactly the same method, the groundings and fans being varied. In the little length reproduced, all the groundings were used. The whole stitch fans can have the leaders twisted to form a line of spaces, and some or all of the passives can be twisted. The half-stitch fans are firmer if the whole stitch is worked at the edge, and they also can have a double whole stitch on the inner edge.

Torchon Edgings Nos. 2 and 3 (Figs. 40 and 42).

These two edgings are put in to show two other edges. The first has a half-stitch edge; the groundwork is Torchon with two twists, and a row of little "spiders" come between it and the edge. It is so easy that it can be worked from the illustration and pricking. The pricking shows where to begin. Nineteen pairs of bobbins were used.

Torchon Edging No. 3.

The only part necessary to explain in this pattern is the fan.

For the complete pattern, 20 pairs of bobbins were used. The

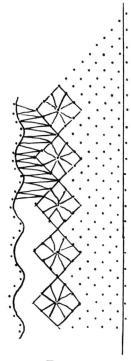

FIG. 39

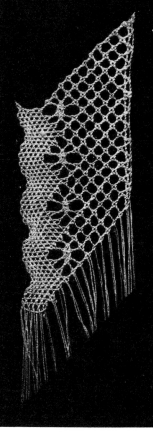

FIG. 40

41

ground stitch is: Twisted half-stitch. The little squares have spiders and the large diamonds are of whole stitch. The six pairs of passives passing from the whole stitch diamond are each twisted twice between the diamonds and fan, and once between the leaders.

FOR THE FAN. Hang two pairs on a pin in pin-hole 1 (Fig. 43). Enclose pin with a whole stitch. The left-hand pair are the edge or

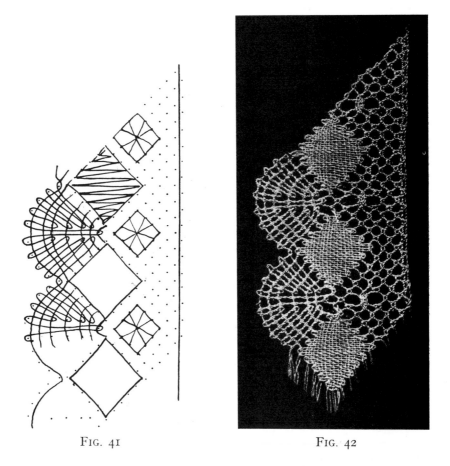

FIG. 41   FIG. 42

outside passives. They are twisted three times between the pin heads, and once at the pin-hole.

The inner pair are the leaders, which are twisted twice between the passives and twice when passing round the pins.

The fan leaders first run at an angle parallel to the side of the whole stitch diamond. They gradually change the angle until they are parallel to the top side of the next diamond.

To Work the Fan. Take the second pair (from left) as leaders through five pairs of passives, twisting twice between each. Twist passives once. Put up pin in hole 2. Enclose pin with whole stitch. Work out to edge, twisting as before. Put up pin in hole 3. Continue thus until pin 9 is enclosed. Bring leaders right up the middle of the fan. Take in the sixth passive (from corner of diamond). Put up pin in hole 10. Work back to 11, and continue to end of fan,

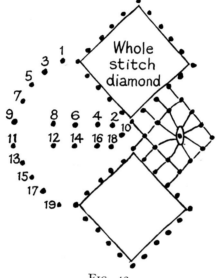

FIG. 43

when pin 19 is enclosed. There should be six passives ready (twisted twice) for the next diamond.

These fans require to be very carefully pulled into position.

Torchon Insertion Sampler (Figs. 44 and 45).

Thirty-four pairs of bobbins are required.

Commence with the ground on the left side. Work the pin-holes from *A* down to *B* (which use 14 pairs). The pairs should be hung in as the work proceeds. Complete the triangular space of ground down to hole *C*. Leave this and work a similar piece of ground on the right-hand side.

FIG. 44   FIG. 45

THE TRAIL. Hang two pairs on a pin at 1. Use one pair as leaders to work whole stitch across and across, hanging a new pair at 2,[1] also at 3, 4, and 5 as you come to them. Leave out pairs at 4, 6, and 8. Take in pairs from the ground on the left side of work, continue to

[1] No. 2 pin-hole is necessary to commence the pattern. It should not be pricked after the first repeat.

44

leave out pairs on the other side of trail, and work on until the trail turns and leave.

Commence the half-stitch trail with the pair from hole 4 and the first one left out from the ground on the right-hand side. Take in pairs from 6 and 8, also those from the right-hand ground. Leave

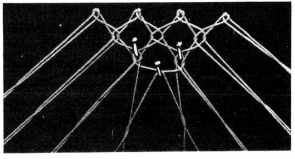

Fig. 46

pairs out on the opposite side of trail; work down to where the trail turns and leave.

Now work the whole of the filling.

Continue the whole stitch trail to the end.

Continue the half-stitch trail until the three pairs from the end of the whole stitch trail have been taken in.

Continue the grounding.

Torchon "Twisted Half-stitch" Ground.

Illustrated in the Torchon sampler, Fig. 30, at 4.

It is pricked and worked diagonally.

To Work. Use two pairs to each pin-hole, twist each

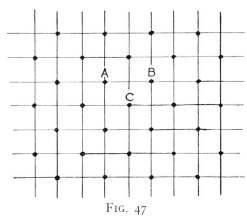

Fig. 47

pair once. With right-hand pair from *A*, and left-hand pair from *B*, make a half-stitch and one extra twist, put up a pin in hole *C*, between the pairs, and enclose with a half-stitch.

45

This same ground with two twists between each pin is illustrated in the Torchon sampler, Fig. 30, in space 7, and with three twists is shown in space 6. The working is as on p. 45.

Torchon Double Ground (*Fig.* 48).

Pricked and worked diagonally (Fig. 47).
Illustrated in the Torchon sampler at 8.

TO WORK. Use two pairs to each pin-hole, twist each pair once. With the right-hand pair from *A* and the left-hand pair from *B* make

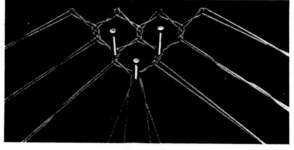

FIG. 48

a whole stitch, twist each pair once (this twist is sometimes left out, but it makes the stitch firmer), put up a pin in hole *C* between the pairs, and enclose with a whole stitch and one twist.

Torchon Spider (*Fig.* 50).

This stitch or filling is made in a little square space placed diamondwise in the groundwork. It can be seen in the Torchon sampler, Fig. 30, at No. 17.

THE PRICKING. When making the pricking the groundwork holes are omitted and one hole is made in the middle of the space instead (Fig. 49).

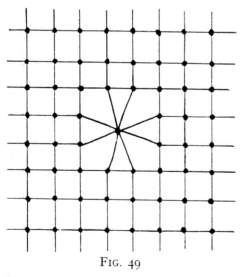

FIG. 49

46

The one illustrated by Fig. 50 has eight "legs," but it can be larger if desired.

To Work the Spider. The four upper pairs from the groundwork are each twisted three times, then those on the left side pass through those on the right in whole stitch. A pin is put up in the centre hole, the four pairs are pulled into position, and then the

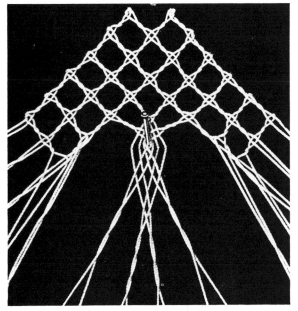

FIG. 50

threads all crossed again in whole stitch, twisting each three times before being taken into the groundwork.

Twisted Spider.

Illustrated in the Torchon sampler, Fig. 30, space 17.

The spider may be varied by twisting each pair between the whole stitches.

Plaits used in Torchon Lace (Fig. 52).

In Torchon lace, plaits can be used either as a powdering in a groundwork, as a filling, or clustered to form little stars, flowers, leaves, etc.

They can be seen in the Torchon sampler, Fig. 30, No. 11 and 14, spotting the ground, and in 12 and 13 also spotting the ground, but worked parallel to it.

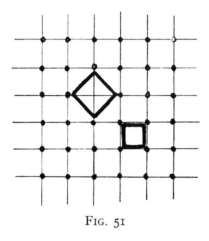

In filling No. 24 they are clustered at No. 15 and 16.

The method of working is described in the general notes No. 12.

The enlarged diagram shows the two angles at which it can be made when spotting a ground (Fig. 51).

Any grounding can be used and spots arranged in many ways.

Raised plaits (General Notes, Fig. 20), are sometimes used in Torchon. When four plaits cross in the centre, the two upper ones have a whole stitch at their lower ends and are then crossed as the windmill in whole stitch. Two whole stitches should follow the crossing before making the other plaits.

FIG. 51

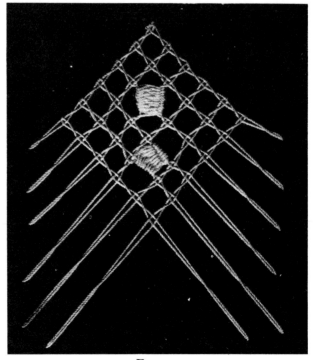

48

FIG. 52

For crossing more than four plaits, explanation is given in directions for Cluny lace, in which they more frequently occur.

Torchon "Rose" Grounds or Fillings.

There are many arrangements of Torchon stitches, all of which are suitable for use for grounding or filling smaller spaces.

Of these stitches, the "Rose" varieties are the best known.

In some localities they are called "Fours."

They are mostly pricked and worked in sets of four holes to complete one "Rose" or repeat.

In the diagrams these stitches are treated as "fillings," the red thread indicating the line where the ordinary grounding ends.

Rose Ground or Filling No. 1.

Illustrated in the Torchon sampler, Fig. 30, space 25 (Fig. 54).

THE PRICKING. This is the same as an ordinary Torchon ground,

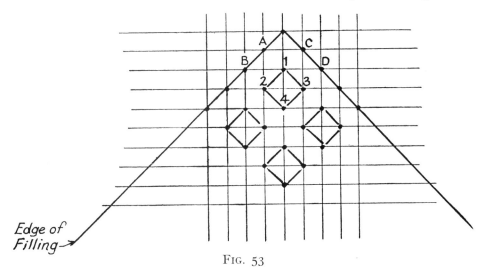

FIG. 53

with the addition of little lines drawn on the pattern to group the holes into sets of four, as in Fig. 53.

TO WORK THE GROUND OR FILLING. Four pairs of bobbins are necessary for each rose. Twist each pair once, make a half-stitch (no pin), leave.

49

* With the two middle pairs make a half-stitch. Put up a pin in hole 1. Enclose pin with a half-stitch.

With the two left-hand pairs make a half-stitch. Put up a pin in hole 2. Enclose pin with a half-stitch.

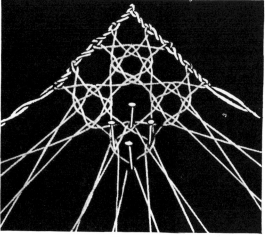

FIG. 54

With two right-hand pairs make a half-stitch. Put up a pin in hole 3. Enclose pin with a half-stitch.

With two middle pairs make a half-stitch. Put up a pin in hole 4. Enclose with a half-stitch.

Now with the two left-hand pairs make a half-stitch (no pin); leave. Do the same with the two right-hand pairs. Continue from *, dropping two of the pairs just worked and using the two next pairs instead.

Rose Ground or Filling No. 2.

Illustrated in the Torchon sampler, Fig. 30, space 26.

THE PRICKING. This is the same as for filling No. 1, with the addition of a hole between each set of four holes, as the pricking in Fig. 55 shows.

TO WORK THE FILLING. The four holes grouped together are worked exactly the same as for filling No. 1. The difference is the addition of the pin and extra stitch between the groups. This intervening stitch, or crossing, is made by a half-stitch. Put up the pin in the between hole. Enclose pin with a half-stitch.

50

Torchon Rose Ground or Filling No. 3.

Illustrated in Torchon sampler, Fig. 30, space 18. The middle space of the insertion and in Fig. 57.

THE PRICKING is exactly the same as No. 1 filling, Fig. 53.

There are three varieties of this filling. In each kind the group of four holes is worked the same, the difference being in the

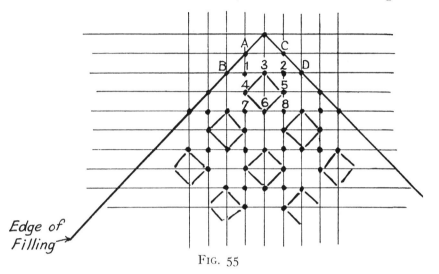

FIG. 55

stitch between the groups. The one illustrated in Fig. 56 is the best.

TO WORK THE FILLING. With two pairs from *A* and *B*, twisted twice, make a half-stitch, and one extra twist. Do the same with the two pairs from *C* and *D*.

Now work the group of holes with the four pairs just used.

With the two middle pairs make a half-stitch and one extra twist. Put up a pin in hole 1. Enclose pin with a half-stitch and one extra twist.

With the two left-hand pairs

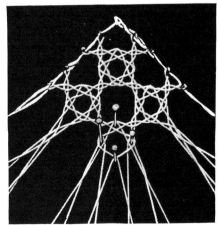

FIG. 56

51

make a half-stitch and one extra twist. Put up a pin in hole 2. Enclose pin with a half-stitch and one extra twist. With the two right-hand pins make a half-stitch and one extra twist. Put up a pin

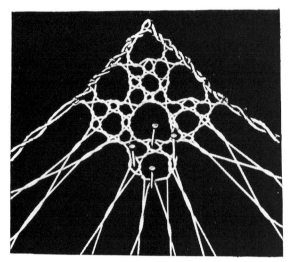

FIG. 57

in hole 3. Enclose pin with a half-stitch and one extra twist. With the two middle pairs make a half-stitch and one extra twist. Put up a pin in hole 4. Enclose pin with a half-stitch and one extra twist. A half-stitch and extra twist are used between each group of holes. The variety used in the middle of the insertion, page 44, has only a half-stitch between the groups, without the extra twist before and after it.[1] The variety used in the Torchon sampler, Fig. 30, at 18 is not often satisfactory, owing to it having two half-stitches with extra twists

between the groups. This makes it kink when the pins are removed. It is suitable if very fine thread is used, but the other stitches must be carefully chosen or they will look thin and stringy.

Torchon Rose Ground or Filling No. 4.

Illustrated in the top middle space of the insertion, page 44.

THE PRICKING is the same as No. 1 filling (Fig. 53).

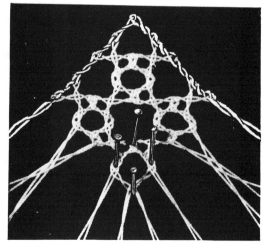

FIG. 58

[1] This filling is occasionally used in " Bucks Point."

To Work the Filling. It is worked in a similar way to No. 1 filling. The intervening stitches consist of a whole stitch with one

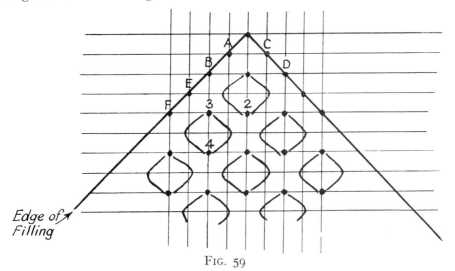

Fig. 59

twist before and after it. For the groups of four holes, each pin has a whole stitch and one twist before it and a whole stitch and one twist after it. This stitch requires more care in "pulling up" than many others.

Torchon Rose Ground or Filling No. 5 (*Fig.* 60).

Illustrated in the Torchon sampler, Fig. 30, space 20.

The Pricking. Similar to filling No. 1. The side holes of the groups are not pricked, but indicated by lines on the pattern (Fig. 53).

To Work the Filling. Use four pairs, from *A*, *B*, *C*, and *D*.

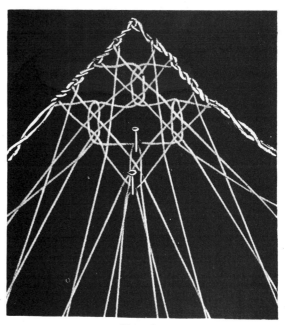

Fig. 60

53

With each pair twisted once, make a half-stitch leave.

* With the two middle pairs make a half-stitch. Put up a pin into hole 1.

Enclose pin with half-stitch.

With the two left-hand pairs make a half-stitch.

With the two right-hand pairs make a half-stitch.

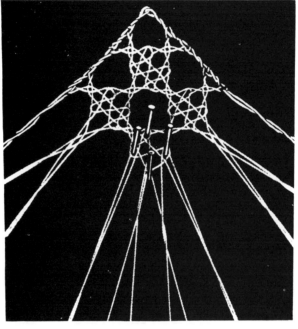

Fig. 61

With the two middle pairs make a half-stitch. Put up a pin in hole 2.

Enclose pin with half-stitch.

With the two left-hand pairs make a half-stitch.

With the two right-hand pairs make a half-stitch.

Repeat from *, hole 3 being like hole 1.

Torchon Closed Check Ground or Filling No. 6 (*Fig.* 61).

Illustrated in the Torchon sampler, Fig. 30, space 23.

THE PRICKING. Is the same as filling No. 2 (having extra holes between groups) (Fig. 55).

54

To Work the Filling. Use four pairs from *A*, *B*, *C*, and *D*.

With each two pairs twisted once, make a half-stitch. Put up pins in the intervening holes 1 and 2. Enclose pins with half-stitch and leave. Now work the group of holes with the same four pairs just used. With the two middle pairs, make a half-stitch, giving one extra twist to the right-hand pair. Put up a pin in hole 3. Enclose pin with half-stitch.

With the two left-hand pairs, make a half-stitch, giving one extra twist to the outside pair. Put up a pin in hole 4. Enclose pin with

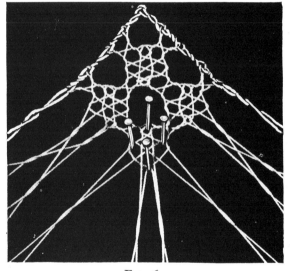

Fig. 62

a half-stitch. Make a half-stitch with the two middle pairs (to close the centre of the "rose").

With the two right-hand pairs make a half-stitch, giving an extra twist to the outside pair. Put up a pin in hole 5. Enclose pin with half-stitch.

With the two middle pairs make a half-stitch, giving an extra twist to the right-hand pair. Put up a pin in hole 6. Enclose pin with a half-stitch.

In between each group make a half-stitch. Put up a pin. Enclose pin with half-stitch.

Torchon " Closed Check " Ground or Filling No. 7 (Fig. 62).

These "Closed check" fillings have the "rose" or group of four holes filled with a stitch instead of being left open.

Illustrated in the Torchon sampler, Fig. 30, space 19.

THE PRICKING is the same as No. 1 filling (Fig. 53).

TO WORK THE FILLING. Use four pairs from *A*, *B*, *C*, and *D*.

With each two pairs twisted twice, make a half-stitch and one extra twist, leave.

Now work the group of holes with four pairs just used.

With the two middle pairs make a half stitch, and one extra twist.

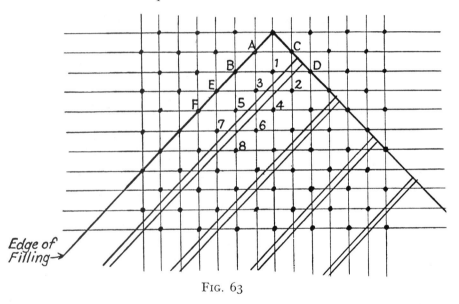

FIG. 63

Put up a pin in hole 1. Enclose pin with a half-stitch.

With the two left-hand pairs make a half-stitch, twisting outside pair twice and inner pair once. Put up a pin in hole 2, but do not enclose. Do the same with the two right-hand pairs, using pin-hole 3. Make a half-stitch with the two middle pairs (this closes the centre of the rose). Now enclose pins 2 and 3 with a half-stitch, giving an extra twist to the outside pair.

With the two middle pairs, make a half-stitch and one extra twist. Put up a pin in hole 4. Enclose pin with a half-stitch, twisting twice.

56

A half-stitch with an extra twist is used between each group of holes.

Torchon Ground or Filling No. 8 (Fig. 64).

This ground or filling and those following are worked in lines diagonally.

THE PRICKING is made like an ordinary Torchon ground. Diagonal lines are drawn on the pricking in the direction in which the pattern is to be worked (Fig. 63).

This variety is illustrated in the Torchon sampler, Fig. 30, space 21.

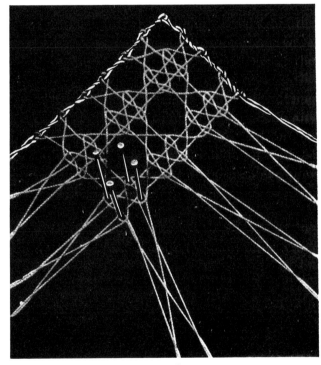

FIG. 64

TO WORK THE FILLING. Use the four pairs from A, B, C, D. Twist each pair once, make a half-stitch, leave.

* With the two middle pairs, make a half-stitch. Put up a pin in hole 1. Enclose pin with half-stitch. Drop the left-hand pair, and with the two right-hand pairs make a half-stitch. Put up a pin in hole 2. Enclose pin with half-stitch. With the two middle pairs make a half-stitch. With the two left-hand pairs make a half-stitch. Put up a pin in hole 3. Enclose pin with half-stitch. With the two middle pairs make a half-stitch. Put up a pin in hole 4. Enclose pin with half-stitch.

With the two left-hand pairs make a half-stitch. *

The two right-hand pairs are left out ready for the next row.[1] For this filling they should be worked together in one twist and half-stitch and left. Take the two pairs on left side and two fresh pairs from *E* and *F*. Repeat from * to * until the row is finished.

Torchon Ground or Filling No. 9 (*Fig.* 65).

Illustrated in the Torchon sampler, Fig. 30, space 29.

THE PRICKING is the same as for No. 8 filling (Fig. 63).

TO WORK THE FILLING. Use the four pairs from *A*, *B*, *C*, and *D*. Those from *A* and *B* should be twisted three times each.

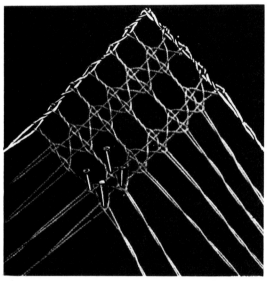

FIG. 65

Those from *C* and *D* twist once and make a half-stitch.

With the two middle pairs make a half-stitch. Put up a pin in hole 1. Enclose pin with half-stitch.

With the two right-hand pairs make a half-stitch. Put up a pin in hole 2. Enclose pin with half-stitch.

With the two middle pairs make a half-stitch.

With the two left-hand pairs make a half-stitch. Put up a pin in hole 3. Enclose pin with half-stitch.

With the two middle pairs make a half-stitch. Put up a pin in hole 4. Enclose pin with half-stitch.

With the two middle pairs make a half-stitch.

Repeat from the beginning until the row is complete.

Each pair is twisted three times between the rows.

[1] It will be seen that in this example the pairs grouped together in half-stitch between the rows come exactly opposite to each other. Another pretty variety of this filling is obtained by alternating them as illustrated in the Torchon sampler, space 22. In this case the first and last pairs are just twisted once before being taken into the next row.

58

TORCHON LACE

Torchon Ground or Filling No. 10 (*Fig.* 66).

Illustrated in the insertion in the lowest middle space.

THE PRICKING is the same as for filling No. 8 (Fig. 63).

TO WORK THE FILLING. It is worked like the last filling (9), except that whole stitches are used instead of half-stitches, one twist being given when passing round a pin. Either two or three

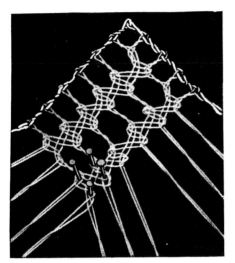

FIG. 66

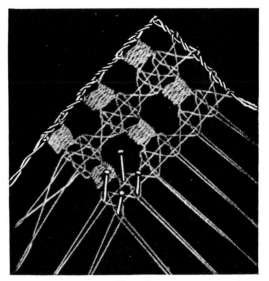

FIG. 67

twists may be used between the rows, but, of course, always using the same number for one filling.

Torchon Ground or Filling No. 11 (*Fig.* 67).

Illustrated in the Torchon sampler, Fig. 30, space 24.

THE PRICKING is the same as for filling No. 8 (Fig. 63).

TO WORK THE FILLING. The rows of half-stitch are exactly the same as No. 8 filling. The pairs between the rows of half-stitch, instead of being twisted are used to make a row of little square plaits (described on page 22).

CHAPTER VI
TORCHON CORNERS

THE advantage of a turned corner is obviously great when compared with the clumsy methods of either frilling the lace on to the linen at the corner or cutting and joining an insertion.

This turning of corners is such a very easy matter that it is surprising to find it so seldom used.

It is not always necessary to add bobbins to turn. The pattern, in most cases, can be worked straight on to a line that cuts diagonally across the pattern where the corner turns. The work is then turned and continued as before from this corner line. When the design is based upon a diagonal stripe, it will be necessary to reverse the pattern in the centre of the side, to avoid the next corner being entirely different.

This reversing, which must, of course, be made in the centre of the side, often adds interest to the design.

Repeating Mirror.

When arranging corners from straight borders, an unframed mirror is a great help. The metal ones are best because they have not the thickness of the glass to be doubled by reflection. This thickness often obscures that part of the pattern most wanted. The mirror is held vertically over the strip of lace, at right angles to the edge if a "reverse" is required, and at an angle of 45 degrees if for a corner. The use of a repeating mirror will show exactly the right line to reverse from. It also gives a general idea of the finished corner, and at the same time, shows if it will be practical in working.

To Work Square Borders.

The corner is commenced or "set in" at about one head, or repeat, before the corner turns. Choose a part of the pattern where there is a natural division in the design.

The bobbins must be wound in pairs, and hung round the pins so that they form the first stitch round each pin (see page 11). A mushroom pillow is useful for turning corners, but not absolutely necessary. When the corner is worked and the edging finished down to the edge of the pricking, it will be necessary to "set up" the work again.

To Set Up. Place a cover cloth under all the bobbins, fold it over (bottom to top) with the bobbins inside it. With two strong pins, one on either side, pin *very* tightly round the bobbins, so that they cannot move and are in a kind of bag. Lift this cloth of bobbins a little and pin it securely to the pillow. This slackens the threads and prevents the lace from drawing up when the pins are removed. Remove all the pins, taking care not to disarrange the lace stitches. Lift the bobbins and lace from the pillow, without letting them loose from the "bag," put them aside carefully (the thread must on no account be pulled). Renew your pricking, and repin the cloth of bobbins to the pillow, so that it is high enough for the lace to come well up over the pricking, and allow the intervening threads to remain loose. Put back sufficient pins to keep the lace well in position (usually about a head and a half). Unpin the bobbins and continue the work. This method is used by lace-makers at the end of each "down" or pricking. A better method for considerable lengths of lace is to make the pricking long enough to fit round the pillow. The pillow can be padded with a strip of flannel until the holes of the pricking exactly fit. An alternative is to make two lengths of pricking. Work to the end of one. Place the other beneath it and continue. Of course, the holes at the top of the one pricking must accurately fit those at the lower end of the other pricking.

To Finish off a Square Border.

When the lace is completed, pin the beginning of the work to the pricking so that the pattern exactly fits. Work from the outside and join each stitch as follows: Insert a fine crochet hook into the loop or first stitch and draw one of the pair of threads through it, forming a loop. Pass the other bobbin through this loop and tie up tightly. The reef knot should be used (see General Notes, page 13).

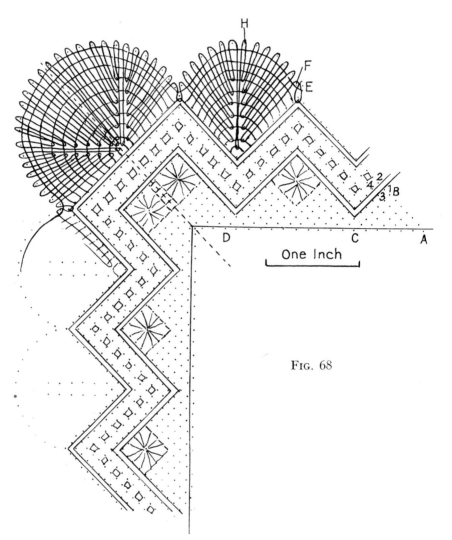

FIG. 68

When all threads are secure, cut off closely.

An insertion is turned at the corner and finished in exactly the same way.

Torchon Corner No. 1.

This is a very easy corner to turn. For both border and corner, 26 pairs of bobbins are sufficient.

62

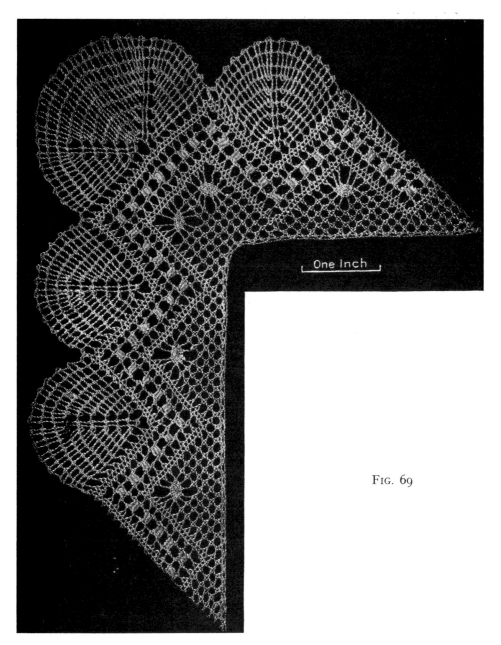

One Inch

Fig. 69

HAND-MADE BOBBIN LACE WORK

The stitches used were : Torchon ground, spiders, half-stitch trails, plaits, and fan edge (see Figs. 68 and 69).

Commence the Torchon ground at hole A, hanging in the pairs as you work. Finish the little triangular-shaped piece of ground from A to B and C. Next work the little half-stitch trail with two pairs of passives and one leader pair. Take in the pairs from the ground on the outer edge, and leave out pairs on the other side.

When arriving at a point in the trail, enclose the extreme pin-hole. Leave the leader pair and use the pair from the other side of the trail as leaders instead. This gains a pin-hole and turns the work. The first two square plaits are made next with the Torchon ground line edging them. The other half-stitch trail follows and is worked like the first one. Take in the two pairs from the first plait. Work three holes of trail, then turn (as explained above). Work down the next length of trail, hanging in pairs on outer edge, and leaving out on inner side. Next make the row of Torchon ground with the six little plaits, and also the half-stitch trail. Fill in the grounding and the little spider down to hole D. Work the two trails and plaits down to the next point and leave.

THE FAN is made next. Hang two pairs round a pin in hole E. Enclose pin with whole stitch. The left-hand pair are the outside or edge passives. The right-hand pair are the leaders. These leaders are taken in to the end pin-hole of trail and dropped out again immediately. Work leaders out through the passives. Twist leaders twice. Put up edge pin in F. The leaders must be twisted twice between each passive pair and the next, also round edge and inner pins. The passives are twisted once between the leaders, except the edge pair, which are twisted three times between the pin-heads and once at the pin-hole. Nine pairs of passives should drop from the passives, each pair twisted twice. Enclose pin F and work leaders through eight passives, twisting twice between each pair and the next. Put up a pin in hole G. Bring leaders out again to edge, still twisting them twice and the passives once. Continue weaving the fan, following the course marked out for the leaders on the pricking. When hole H has been enclosed, bring the leaders right up the middle. Take in the ninth passive from the trail. Put up a pin,

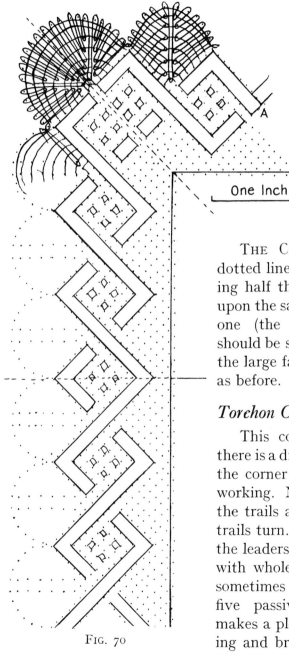

One Inch

FIG. 70

and work leaders out again to edge. Continue to follow the course of the leaders until the fan is complete. The nine passives should each be twisted twice ready to be taken into the trail The leaders will be taken into the end hole of trail and out again at once for next fan.

THE CORNER. Work up to the dotted line crossing the corner, working half the large fan. This is made upon the same principle as the smaller one (the pricking and illustration should be sufficient guide). Complete the large fan and continue the border as before.

Torchon Corner No. 2.

This corner is arranged so that there is a division in the pattern where the corner turns. This simplifies the working. Notice also that leaders of the trails are not changed where the trails turn. This method of changing the leaders is not quite so satisfactory with whole stitch, so the trails have sometimes four and at other times five passives. The centre reverse makes a pleasant change in the working and breaks the monotony of the border.

65

The stitches used were a Torchon ground, whole and half-stitch trails, rose fillings No. 1, a variety of No. 3, and a fan edge. This bordering is so easy that after having worked the last corner it needs

no description beyond the pricking and illustration (Figs. 70 and 71).

The holes in the pricking show exactly where to commence. The hole marked *A* is necessary for commencing, but is not to be pricked elsewhere. Twenty-six pairs of bobbins are required.

Torchon Corner No. 3.

For this corner 27 pairs of bobbins are required, also one pair more to use when necessary in the little half-stitch trail surrounding the filling (Figs. 72 and 73).

STITCHES USED. A twisted half-stitch ground, whole- and half-stitch blocks. Filling of closed check No. 5, with half-stitch trail border, and fan edge. Commence the half-stitch trail which borders

FIG. 71

the filling by hanging two pairs on a pin at hole 1. Use one of these as leader pair, and work across and across, hanging in a pair at each pin-hole 2, 3, 4, and 5.

Bring leaders back through three pairs. Put up a pin in hole 6. Continue the left side of this half-stitch trail, hanging in a new pair at each outer pin-hole, and leaving out pairs on the inner side. When at the point where the trail turns, leave it. Continue the right-hand

66

part of the trail by using the pair left out at hole 6 as the leader pair. Work through two pairs, and hang in a fresh pair at hole 9.

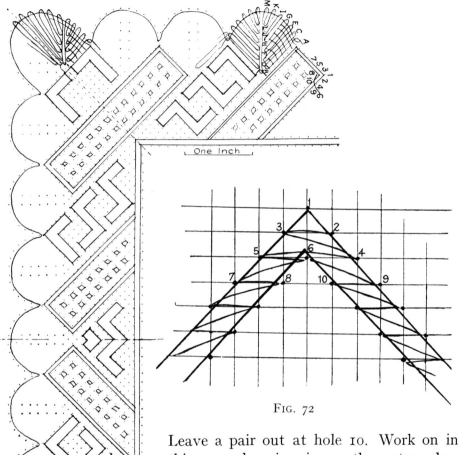

One Inch

FIG. 72

Leave a pair out at hole 10. Work on in this way, hanging in on the outer edge, and leaving out on the inner edge until the trail meets the edge or "foot side." The edge stitches are worked in the usual way. Next, work the whole of the filling and the edge stitches where it meets the "foot side." Return to the unfinished trail. You will find it necessary to hang in the extra pair on the inner side, in order to keep it the right texture (three pairs passives).

67

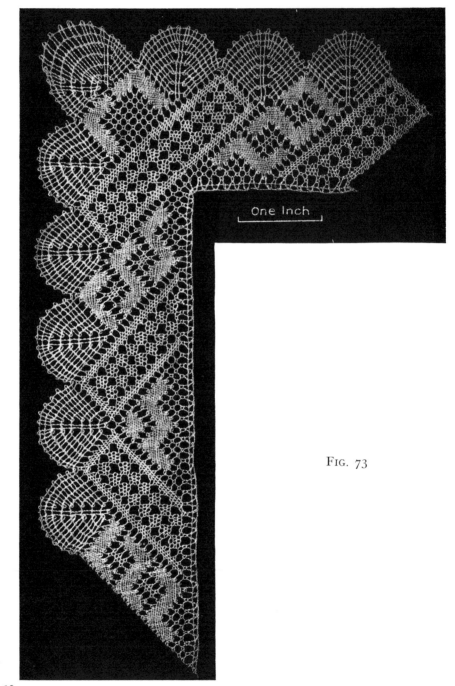

One Inch

FIG. 73

Finish this trail down to the edge. Tie up and take out the extra pair.

THE FAN is made next. Hang two pairs round the pin in hole *A*. Enclose pin with a whole stitch. The left-hand pair will be the edge or outside passive. The right-hand pair are the leaders. Work the fan as explained before. Eight pairs pass from the trail into the fan and out again into the whole stitch-block. These cloth stitch blocks, and half-stitch between, do not need to be described, the pricking and illustration being sufficient guide.

THE CORNER. Work up to the dotted line across the corner. Then continue the large fan. Work the border from the dotted line. To continue the little half-stitch trail, it will be found necessary to turn the direction of the leaders. This is done by leaving the leaders after having enclosed the outside pin. Use the pair on the inner edge instead. This gains a pin-hole and turns the work.

NOTE. When making some of these narrow half-stitch trails, it may be found necessary to put in a new pair of bobbins on the inner side, where the trail turns, thus preventing the trail from becoming too thin. This method can be used instead of reversing the leaders. Both ways are correct, but no definite rule can be laid down. The worker will find it depends partly upon the way the leaders travel at the beginning and partly upon the position of the trail in the design. The extra pair is taken out at the next turn without being noticeable.

Both methods were used in this corner.

CHAPTER VII
EMBROIDERY FINISHINGS

I AM describing a few narrow laces. They are very easy, quickly worked, and effective. For finishing embroideries they are especially useful, as they are workable in cotton, linen, wool, silk, and metal threads, and some or all of the colourings used in the embroidery can be used.

A very slight knowledge of bobbin stitchery is required to enable an embroideress to finish the edges, and make an insertion, braid, edging, cord, or fringe, thus carrying the same individuality through to the completion of the article.

I have given the prickings used for these odd trimmings as a guide to show what holes are necessary. These prickings cannot be taken as proportionately correct, because the laces, being intended for use in conjunction with embroideries, would, of course, be made with the same kind of threads, silk, wool, etc., and in some instances, two kinds (silk and metal). The workers will find that a few trials will give useful results. These trimmings would, of course, be joined to the work with a suitable embroidery stitch worked with the same threads.

No. 1. Cord (Fig. 75).

This can be made in one colour or several colours, and any thickness. It is usually made by two workers plaiting or twisting it with their hands. If able to handle bobbins, one person can easily make it, thereby saving half the time.

To MAKE THE CORD. Hang four threads (or a greater number divided into four groups) round a drawing-pin, which is fixed firmly to a table. Cross the two centre pairs left over right as if commencing an ordinary lace stitch. Hold the bobbins so that they work independently of each other and twist as follows: 2 and 4 change places right over left, then 1 and 3 change places left over right. This is

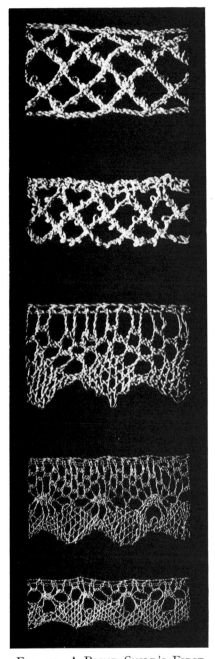

FIG. 74. A BLIND CHILD'S FIRST
PIECES OF LACE

The girl was taught by one of my student
teachers, and shows that bobbin lace need
not be trying to the eyes.

FIG. 75

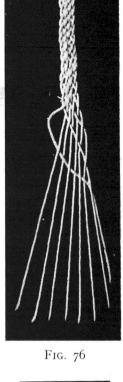

FIG. 76

FIG. 77

FIG. 78

71

only a twist, not a lace stitch. Every twist must be pulled up very tightly.

No. 2. *Braid (Fig. 76).*

This woven braid is especially suitable for bag handles.

Hang eight threads from four pins. Take the end thread on the left side, pass it under and over the others alternately. Pull up closely. Again, take the end thread on the left and weave it under and over the others as before. Any number of threads of uniform thickness can be used and the colouring varied to suit its purpose.

A whole or half-stitch braid made without edge pins also has its uses.

No. 3. *Edging (Figs. 77 and 78).*

Hang three pairs at point *A*. With the two left-hand pairs make a half-stitch plait to *B* and give an extra twist to the outside pair to accentuate the pin-hole. Put up the pin. Enclose pin with a half-stitch plait. With the two right-hand pairs make a whole stitch and a twist. Put up a pin in the next hole. Enclose pin with a whole stitch and one twist, and twist the right-hand pair twice more and leave. Continue by making another plait with the two left-hand pairs.

No. 4. *Insertion (Figs. 79 and 80).*

For this little insertion six pairs of bobbins were used. Each side has a passive pair, and a leader pair which passes round the pins. In the middle are two pairs of another colour, these cross each other, then pass through the outside leaders, round the inner pins, and finally back to the middle. It is not possible to give details of twists, as they must vary to suit the kind of threads used.

No. 5. *Fringe (Figs. 81 and 82).*

Six pairs of bobbins are necessary. The heading consists of a whole stitch braid, the outside passives being twisted between the pins. The leaders are twisted twice to make the pin-holes on left edge. The fringe is made with two pairs, which pass in whole stitch

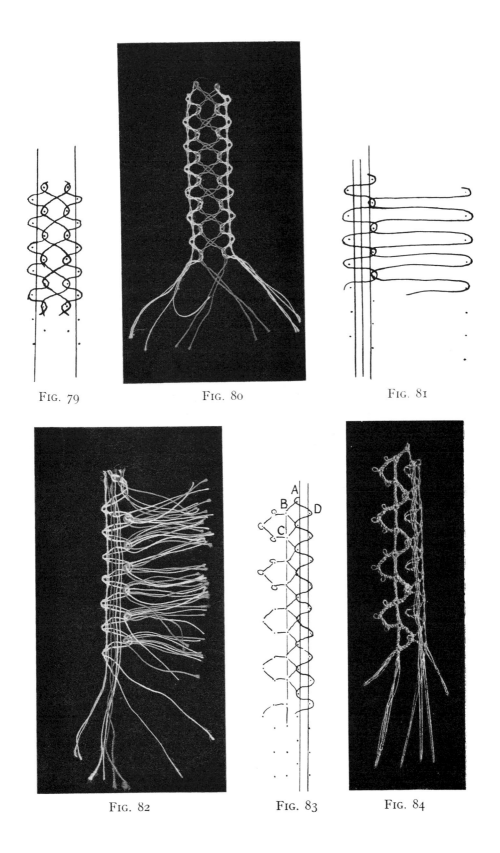

FIG. 79   FIG. 80   FIG. 81

FIG. 82   FIG. 83   FIG. 84

through the leaders. Then, in order to make the fringe secure, they cross each other in whole stitch (which will lie flat if worked in silk or fine thread). The fringe pairs pass out again through the leaders, round the outer pins, and back to the next pin-hole. The long ends are, of course, cut.

No. 6. *Edging* (*Figs.* 83 *and* 84).

This is a "nine-pin" edging. Eight pairs of bobbins were used for it. Hang three pairs at point *A*. With the two pairs on the left-hand side, make a half-stitch plait to *B*. At point *B* hang in two more pairs, crossing all four pairs by making a "windmill" (page 26). The outside pairs make a half-stitch plait with picots on outer edge. The two inner pairs make a plait to *C*, where they again make a windmill. Make plaits to the next pin-holes and leave. Upon the right-hand pair from *A*, which should be twisted twice, hang two passive pairs, then at pin-hole *D* hang in the edge pair. Make an ordinary "foot side" braid taking in and leaving out the half-stitch plaits as indicated by the pricking.

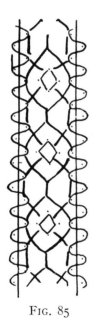

FIG. 85

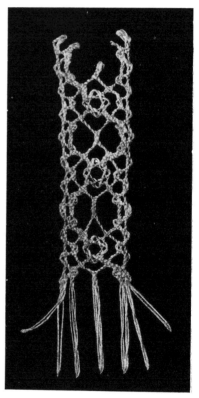

FIG. 86

No. 7. *Insertion* (*Figs.* 85 *and* 86).

This insertion is intended for two kinds of thread, metal and silk. Ten pairs of bobbins are needed, six wound with silk and four with metal. The metal threads make the Torchon "Rose" (Fig. 54), then they make half-stitch plaits, pass through the twisted silk and into the edge leaders, they again plait, and at the next pin-hole pass out again, and through the twisted silk, to make the next "rose." The edge passives and leaders are of silk and so are the diamond-shaped twist that surrounds the "rose," and also the little plaits in between the roses. The diagram clearly shows how the silk should twist, and pass through the metal plaits, into the edge leaders, and out again, so further description is unnecessary.

CHAPTER VIII
CLUNY AND BEDS-MALTESE

CLUNY lace is somewhat similar to Torchon; but it is a little more elaborate, the design is freer, and the lace usually of a coarser texture. Its chief use is for domestic purposes, but for dress requiring heavy trimming it is also suitable. The stitches used are the same as for Torchon, the heavy cloth parts (upon which raised plaits very often occur) are connected by half-stitch plaits or "legs" with single picots. The outer edges are also of plaits with picots.

There are no fresh stitches to explain. Two patterns and prickings are given to show the style of lace. Thread of the coarsest sizes is mostly used, but for some dress purposes, a wool called "Yak" (really wool of Yorkshire sheep) is quite suitable.

Beds-Maltese Lace.

This is the kind of lace which was originally made in Malta, but is now largely made in the Bedfordshire and other Midland villages. It is not unlike a fine Cluny lace.

Unfortunately, much is made of an inferior cotton "slip thread." Some, however, is made of linen, and silk has also found favour. It is chiefly used for personal wear. As no fresh stitches occur, an edging and corner are all that is necessary to show the style of lace.

Cluny Edging (Figs. 87 and 88).

For this edging, 19 pairs of bobbins were used. The pricking was made on eight to the inch sectional paper. No. 35 thread was used. First make the triangular piece of "rose" ground from 1 to 2, and 3.

For the whole stitch diamond, hang three pairs at 4, use the left-hand pair as leaders, and work to 5, where another pair must be hung in. Work to 6 and again hang in a pair. Continue the weaving, taking in the ground pairs at 7 and 9 and hanging in one pair at 8.

FIG. 87

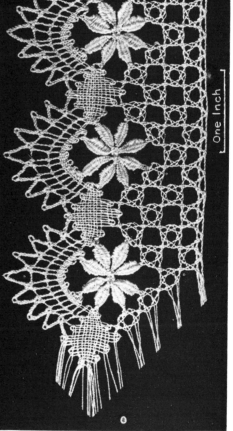

FIG. 88

At 10, two pairs are hung in and left out again at once to make a "leg." At 9 and 11 leave out pairs for the ground. At 13 and 15 leave out pairs for plait *A*. At 12 and 14, leave out pairs, to use as passives; for the fan twist each pair twice. At 15, three pairs should be left, one of which is worked into plait *A*. The middle pair are leaders, and the others are passive. For the fan, the leader pair twists three times between the passive pairs. The inner passive pair twists twice between the leaders, the outer passives twist three times between the pin-holes, and once at the pin-hole. Work the leaders of

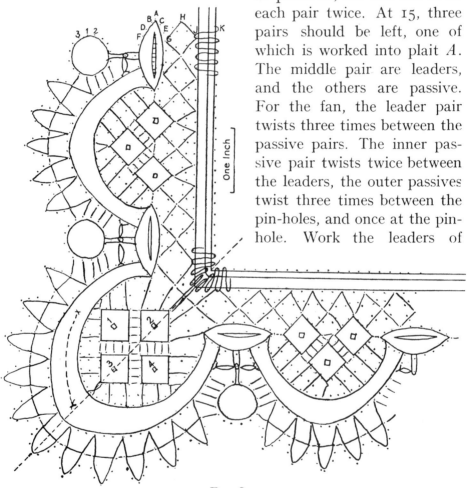

FIG. 89

fan out to the edge at pin-hole 16, make a "windmill" (see General Notes, page 26) with these leaders, the outside passives, and the two pairs from the "leg." With the two outside pairs, make a "leg" to 17, where, instead of the usual picot, an extra twist given to the outside pair, accentuates the pin-hole, and then make a "leg" back to the next pin-hole and leave. The two inner pairs from the "wind-mill" are crossed in whole stitch, then twisted three times each, using the right-hand pair as leaders to continue the fan.

Next work plait *A*. Continue the groundwork, and work plaits *B* and *C*. Now take the pairs from plait *C*, and using the pairs as one bobbin, work them in whole stitch, through those from *B* and *A*. Twist the double pairs from *B* and *A* once right over left, put up a pin in the centre hole to keep them in posi-

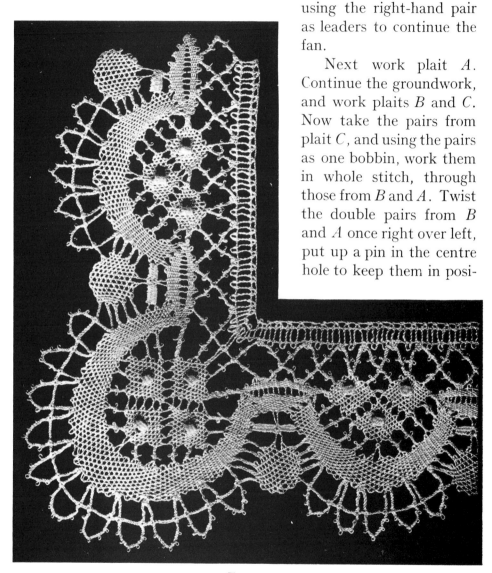

FIG. 90

tion, and leave. Now, with the two pairs woven through from *C*, make plait *D* and take the bobbins from it, into the fan. Continue

79

the fan up to plait E, for which two pairs are left out. Make plait E, which (although rather troublesome to get into position) can be done by raising the plait from the pillow while pulling it up in order to be clear of the pin-heads. The pairs from plait E are next woven back through those from the other plaits in the same way as before. Plait F is next made and the pairs are taken into the whole stitch diamond. After this, make plait G, and then H, which complete the pattern, when taken into the ground.

Cluny Corner (Figs. 89 and 90).

Thirty-one pairs of bobbins are necessary for the edging. Eight pairs extra to turn the corner.

The pricking was made on 12 to the inch sectional paper. No. 35 thread was used.

Commence the block of whole stitch which has leaders twisted to form an open vein. Hang three pairs at A, make whole stitch to B, and there hang in two pairs, work across to C and back through three pairs. Here the leaders commence the vein twists. Work to D and hang in two pairs and work to E, then to F, hanging in two pairs, and then work the leaders across to G, and leave. At H, hang in four pairs, make two "legs" with picots as marked on pattern. The left-hand pairs are taken in at G and left out again at once; the right-hand pairs are taken into the "footing" at J, where one pair is hung in as leaders. Next, hang two pairs of passives on to the leaders. The passives always twist once. The leaders twist three times between the passives, and twice when passing round the pins. At K, hang in the edge pair, and twist them three times between each pin. Continue the "foot" side, taking in and leaving out "legs" as shown on the pattern, when six or seven of the edge holes are worked, leave.

Now commence the half-stitch circle, hang two pairs from each of the two top holes, 1 and 2, use one of these as leaders and work across and across in half-stitch, hanging in two pairs at the two next holes (one on each side). The next and last two pairs are hung in on the next pin-hole on the inner or trail side.

When half the circle is finished, a twisted pair is left out. The leaders from the whole stitch block twist and come out, these two pairs pass through two pairs (either from a plait or just hung in), then make a whole stitch. Put up a pin in the middle. Enclose pin with whole stitch, and take the two pairs out again, twist them; the left-hand pair goes into the half-stitch circle, and the right-hand pair goes to work the whole stitch block. Make a plait with the two pairs from the middle of these twisted pairs.

NOTE. This double twisting instead of a leg is used to connect two parts of the lace, the advantage being that neither part gains nor loses bobbins, a condition which would happen if a half-stitch plait or "leg" were made. This also occurs in Beds-Maltese lace. Finish the whole stitch block and half-stitch circle, leaving out (or taking in) pairs as the pricking directs.

At the foot of the whole stitch block, three pairs remain, these make a leg (work whole stitch with the two right-hand pairs, and a whole stitch with the two left-hand pairs alternately).

The half-stitch trail is commenced next with eight pairs from the whole stitch block, the right-hand pair being used as leaders, work the trail to the middle where a single pair is left out, taken into the diamond and back into the trail. It will be necessary to reverse the leaders, so as to gain a pin. This is explained in Torchon (page 67).

Leave the trail and make the half-stitch diamonds, for which the pricking is sufficient guide.

FOR THE CORNER. Continue as for the edging, work about a quarter of the trail and leave it. Now commence the diamond No. 1 at the top of which a new pair must be hung in, and tied out at the foot of No. 4 diamond.

When half No. 1 diamond is finished, continue the trail, putting in new bobbins as it gets too open. From X to X requires seven pairs which should be put in on the outer edge, but can be tied out on both sides after passing the middle. About the middle it will be necessary to reverse the leaders to gain a pin. The pattern can now be completed without further explanation.

Beds-Maltese Edging (Figs. 91 and 92).

For this edging, 22 pairs of bobbins were used wound with No. 4 slip thread.

The pricking was drawn out upon 16 to the inch sectional paper.

Commence with the foot side. Hang two pairs at *A* (one for the edge and one leader pair), upon the leaders hang two pairs of passives. At *B* hang in two pairs, which are left out again to work a "leg"

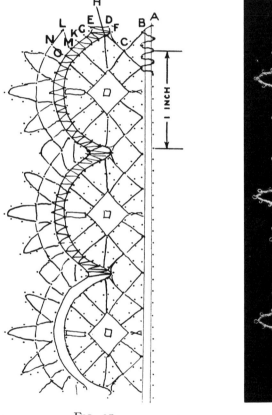

FIG. 91

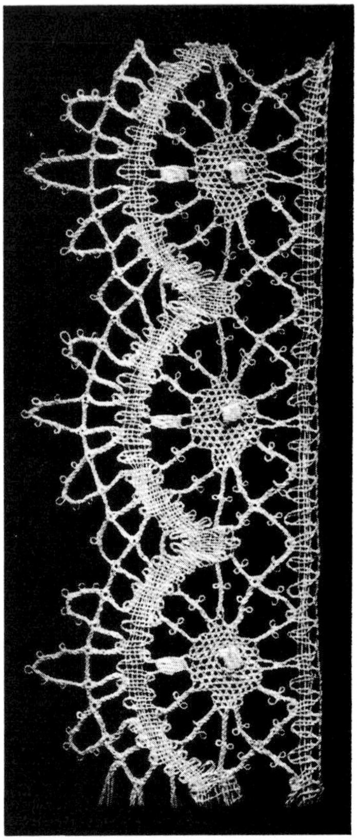

FIG. 92

to *C*, where later a "windmill" will be made with the leg from *F*, work until about four edge holes are made, then leave.

The whole stitch trail is now commenced with seven passive pairs, and a pair of leaders on the right-hand side at *D*. Work to *E* and back to *F*. After enclosing pin in *F*, leave out a pair, work to *G*, then to *H*; when *H* is enclosed leave out three pairs. These with the pair left out from *F* make two "legs," one to *G* and the other to

82

the top of the half-stitch diamond. Continue the trail; when at K, hang in two pairs, and at L hang in four pairs, with which make two "legs," one will travel round the edge, the other will be taken in to the trail at M. At N, hang in two pairs and with them make a "leg" to O. Continue the edge and the trail to the middle of the pattern, leaving out the four pairs on opposite side of trail as indicated by the pricking. Now commence the half-stitch diamond with the two pairs from the leg immediately above, work across and across in half-stitch, taking in the pairs from the trail and foot side.

When half the diamond is finished the leaders come out from left side, and make a plait with a pair left out of the trail, then one pair goes back to continue the diamond and the other is taken into the trail again. On the other side of diamond a little treble twist is made and pairs are crossed to connect with the foot side instead of a "leg" (see Cluny Corner, Fig. 90). A raised plait can be made on the diamond or not. For this see Torchon (Fig. 20). It should be easy to complete the pattern from the pricking and illustration.

Where the trail turns, a pin-hole can be gained by using the leaders and the end passive pair, to make the last "leg" left out instead of putting up a pin as usual, then the end passive pair is taken across as leaders. The "leg" is, of course, taken in again in a similar manner.

Beds-Maltese Corner (Figs. 93 and 94).

This corner is suitable for a handkerchief.

Twenty pairs of bobbins and two extra pairs for corner are necessary. No. 6 slip thread was used. The pricking was drawn upon 16 to the inch sectional paper. Leaders twist twice when passing round the pins. Hang three pairs at A, and use the left-hand pair as leaders, work whole stitch through two pairs (these two pairs drop out and make a "leg' to F). Now hang two passive pairs upon the leaders and also hang in a pair at the edge pin B, work two more foot braid holes and leave.

Hang three pairs at C (for the edge), twist right-hand pair three

times and leave ready to be taken into the trail, with the two left-hand pairs make a "leg" to D, where two more pairs must be added and "legs" made for the outer edges.

At E hang two pairs twisted twice and enclose the pin with whole stitch. These pairs are the leaders for the trails. On the right-hand leader hang three pairs of passives and one more pair (this will come through the trail and work into a "leg" for the centre). Twist the leaders four times and work them through the pairs from the leg at A. Put up a pin in F, twist leaders twice and bring them round pin, then again through the "leg" pairs, twist four times and leave. Make the "leg" from F, and take it into the footing, leave the pairs out again, make another "leg" with them and leave.

Upon the left-hand trail leaders (hung in at E) hang two passive pairs and the extra pair (for the centre "leg") put up a pin in G, twist leaders twice round pin and leave.

There will now be seven pairs between the two

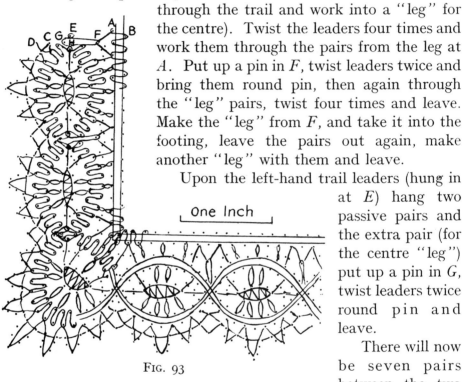

One Inch

FIG. 93

leader pairs. Of these seven pairs, take the fourth from the left through three pairs to the right in whole stitch, then bring the third pair through three pairs, then the second pair through three pairs and also the first pair through three pairs. This crosses the trails. Pull all up tightly. Bring the right-hand leaders back through four pairs and leave. Bring the left-hand leaders through three pairs and leave. Cross the leader pairs in whole stitch, twist twice, put up a pin in hole H and cover with whole stitch. Work the right-hand leaders through four pairs, put up a pin in the next outside hole, work back through

84

three pairs, leaving the fourth for the centre "leg." Work the left-hand leaders through three pairs, put up a pin in the next outside hole, work back through two pairs leaving the third for the centre "leg." Work out again through two pairs, take in the twisted pair from C, and leave. The centre "leg" can now be made, and the trails, edge, and "foot" side, and the centre whole stitch block continues. The wide plaits connecting the different parts are made with the two pairs of leaders, the pins being put up before the plait is commenced. Plaits are described in General Notes, page 22, and the little connecting crosses of twisted threads in Cluny Corner (page 80). There is no difficulty with the corner,

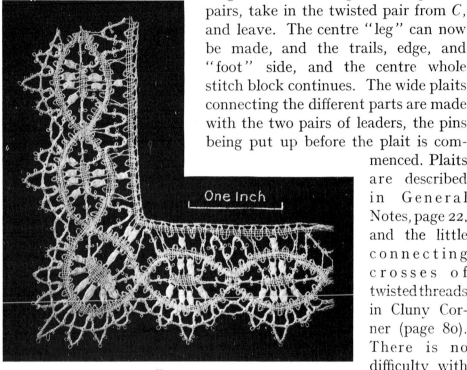

One Inch

FIG. 94

which could be made without adding bobbins. The two pairs are put in only to make the whole stitch block thicker; they are hung in at the top and tied out at the end of block, thereby making no difference to the method of working.

CHAPTER IX
HONITON LACE

HONITON is the finest of the English laces. Unlike the other laces in this book, the design is worked independently of the grounding. The threads do not travel across the design, and then into the ground-work. For this reason, the designing is not so limited and fewer bobbins are required, because each little section can be finished as the work proceeds. Those parts that touch should be connected in the working. The pillow made ground (whether net or pearl pin bars) and the fancy stitches called "fillings," are worked in afterwards. Sometimes sprays are applied to a machine-made net when, of course, the design is of a lighter character, and although pretty is a cheaper style of work and not strictly speaking hand-made. The best work is mostly "raised," that is, outlined with either a raised line of stem stitch, or threads "rolled" along the edge. Needle-made grounding is not desirable for Honiton lace. It takes from the character of the work.

One great advantage this lace has over the "Bucks point" is that the "passive" threads curve in the required direction. This helps the form and is much more artistic than the straight-woven texture of Bucks point ground. Unfortunately, Honiton lace has a "wrong side," which limits its use; otherwise it is suitable for Ecclesiastical or other dress purposes where fine lace is required.

Honiton lace is always made face downwards. This enables the worker to arrange any knots and finishings neatly, so that they do not show on the right side, and often allows her to carry the threads from one part to another without cutting off; which is a great advantage. In the case of raised work it is necessary to work the raised part first.

Before commencing Honiton lace, the student should have read all the general notes and methods which apply to all laces. Before working a sampler, it may be advisable to practice a few stitches and methods for the flat kind of lace. For this I suggest a little piece of braid, which should curve in various ways and vary in width. It can contain fancy holes; also a few simple leaves and

One Inch

FIG. 95

flower forms may be attempted. Figs. 97 and 98 give some simple forms which are suitable for working in various ways. A sampler should contain braid stitches, leaves and flowers, groundings, and

FIG. 96

fillings. Besides being interesting to work, a sampler is excellent practice, and of great use for reference.

Before designing Honiton lace, reference should be made to good specimens of this lace, and also to Brussels and Flemish pillow-made laces from which Honiton was derived.

88

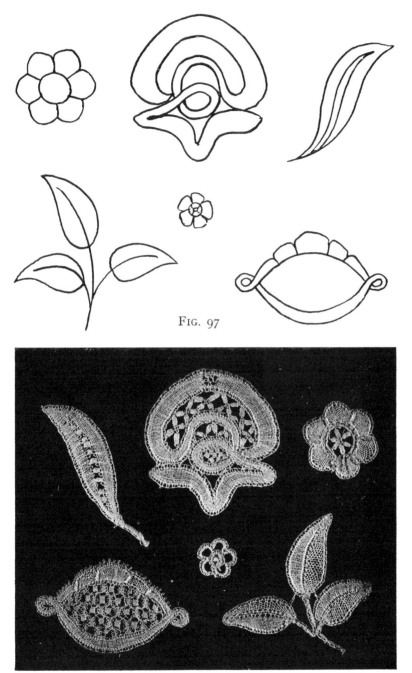

FIG. 97

FIG. 98

Your design must be workable and should strictly adhere to the style of lace. Do not copy that kind of "Honiton lace" which consists of dozens of little sprigs and various odd bits worked separately and joined together in a meaningless way.

Honiton Threads.

A cotton thread is used for Honiton lace-making.

"Old Honiton" was often made of linen, but the use of it seems to have died out, which, for some reasons, is a pity. Cotton produces a softer lace.

The cotton varies in quality and the sizes of the commoner qualities are not dependable; also it is rough, fluffy, and breaks quickly, therefore is not economical.

As regards sizes, no fixed rule can be given. No. 10 skip is very good to begin with and the worker can gradually use finer and finer; 14 skip gives excellent result, but the skips number up to $(27\frac{1}{2})$.

Gimp is a shiny thread of flax. The sizes most suitable for Devon laces are from 24 to 36, according to the size of the skip thread used.

HONITON SAMPLER STITCHES

Sampler space	BRAID STITCHES	Page
1.	Whole stitch "clothing" . .	92
2.	Half-stitch . . .	92
3.	Mittens (vein of leaf) .	94
4.	Plain hole . . .	93
5.	Four pin bud . . .	94
6.	Six pin bud . . .	95
7.	Six pin bud (another) .	95
8.	Twisted leaders . .	105
9.	Zigzag holes . . .	95

Sampler space	LEAVES AND FLOWERS	Page
10.	Half and whole stitch with vein of sewings . . .	105
11.	Raised leaf worked in sections called "taps" . .	107
11a.	Raised flower . .	110
12.	Serrated whole stitch leaf vein of ten stick and cutworks .	108
13.	Whole stitch with vein of "mittens" . . .	105
14.	Whole and half-stitch with vein of cutworks and winkie pins .	106
15.	Half-stitch with raised veins .	109

Sampler space	GROUNDINGS	Page
16.	Purl pin bars . . .	111
17.	Point d'Angleterre net .	113
18.	Trolly net . . .	112

Sampler space	FILLINGS	Page
19.	Cutwork, or leadwork (in flower of ten stick) . .	115
20.	Diamond . . .	115
21.	Brick . . .	117
22.	Pin . . .	118
23.	Cushion . .	119
24.	No pin . . .	120
25.	Toad in the hole . .	121
26.	Blossom . .	123
27.	A swing and a pin . .	125
28.	Point d'Esprit . .	127
29.	Pearl . . .	127
30.	Double ground . .	129
31.	Double ground with cutwork .	130
32.	Bars and cutworks . .	130
33.	Bars and cutworks with hole .	115
34.	Cartwheel . . .	115

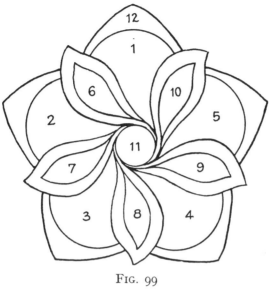

FIG. 99

FIG. 100

Number of space   STITCHES IN THE SMALL HONITON SAMPLER   *Page*

1. Whole stitch blocks 132
2. Cutwork and pinhole 133
3. Cutwork with a hole and a pin 135
4. Four pin blocks 135
5. A variety of " Toad in the hole " 137
6. A variety of " whole stitch block " 133
7. Whole stitch net and cutworks 138
8. Cutwork with a hole in a twisted net 139
9. Cutwork and lattice 139
10. Whole stitch net and cutworks (another) 138
11. Trolly net and cutworks, or Point d'Esprit 127
12. Five pinhole in braid 95

The Small Honiton Sampler.

This little sampler was worked to show various fillings that are absent from the larger sampler. Although these fillings are to be seen in old historical examples, they are not frequently used.

Honiton Clothing.

The heavy part of Honiton, sometimes called clothing, is woven in the same way as a braid. (See General Notes (page 20).) Three twists are given to the couples for the edge stitches. Whole stitch is mostly employed, but half-stitch is very useful for lighter effects.

Half-stitch is indicated in a pricking by two holes pricked close together in the middle of the space where it is to be worked. In clothing, bobbins can be added or cut out as the shape requires, the threads being woven to the various shapes of the design.

Honiton Braid Stitches.

Very few varieties of fancy stitches are allowed in Honiton cloth work. Those described must be very sparingly used.

Whole stitch is occasionally broken by lines, which are formed by the leaders being twisted between the passive pairs (see Honiton sampler, Fig. 95, space 8). The passives may be twisted in a similar manner. The passives can be grouped by means of a whole stitch being made with each set of four threads. These twistings can be seen in the Victoria and Albert Museum, Lace, No. T69—1913.

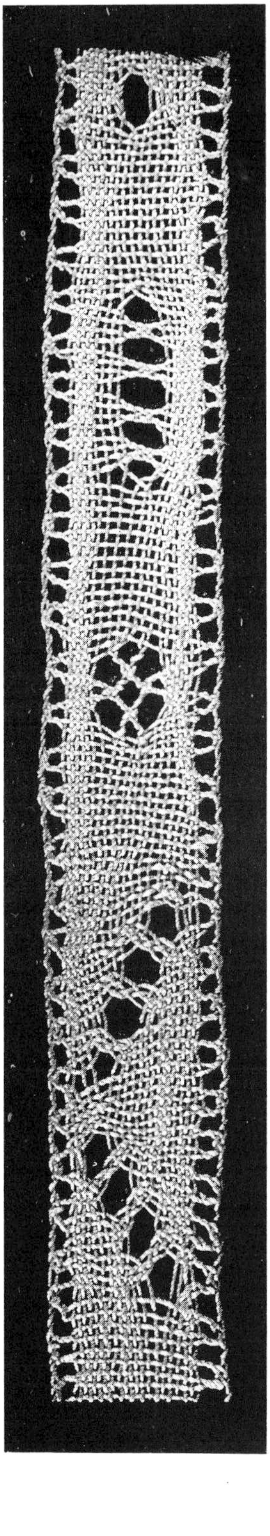

No. 1. *Plain Hole.*

Illustrated in the Honiton sampler, Fig. 95 (4), and in the enlarged braid at top of Fig. 101. Workers use a pinhole in their pricking to denote where this hole is to be made, although it is not used in the working. Leave the leaders at the edge. Divide the bobbins into two equal parts and with the two middle pairs make a half-stitch (this opens the hole). Bring the leaders through to the middle, and with the nearest pair from the centre half-stitch make a turning stitch, that is, a whole stitch and one twist, then cross the two middle threads left over right. Work out to the edge again, make the usual pinhole, enclose the pin, leaving the leaders as the third pair.

OPPOSITE SIDE. Use the other pair from the centre half-stitch as leaders, work out to the edge, and make the pinhole, enclose the pin, and work back again to the middle, twist the leaders once, also twist the end pair of passives on the opposite side once, and cross the two middle threads left over right (this is a reversed half-stitch and closes the hole). Find the old leaders (third pair from edge) and continue weaving the braid.

Plain Hole in Curved Braid.

Use the method explained above, but always leave the leaders on the *inner* side of the curve when commencing. If the curve requires it, the leaders on the outer edge can be taken across to the middle two or more times. Do not make these holes very large.

This method is very useful for turning sharp corners.

93

FIG. 101

2. *Mittens*.

This stitch is useful as a fancy braid or as a veining for a leaf. The edge holes should be pricked opposite each other. It can be seen in the Victoria and Albert Museum lace No. 570—1905, and is illustrated in the Honiton sampler, Fig. 95 (3), and in the enlarged braid (Fig. 101) at (2). Leave the leaders on the outside. Divide the pairs by making a half-stitch with the two middle pairs. Bring the leaders through to the middle, twist them twice, and leave. Take the other pair from the centre half-stitch as leaders, out to the edge, put up pin, enclose it, working back to the middle, twist leaders twice, then work the two centre (leader) pairs together in whole stitch and two twists. Take each leader pair out to opposite edge, make the pinholes, and work back again to the middle. Continue these little centre crossings as far as required, leave the leaders each as third pair from the edge, close middle passives by making a reversed half-stitch (twist two middle pairs once, then cross two middle threads left over right), then continue weaving the braid, using the leaders from the opposite side to the next pinhole.

3. *"Four-pin Bud."*

This hole and similar holes are to be seen in the Victoria and Albert Museum, lace No. 699–68.

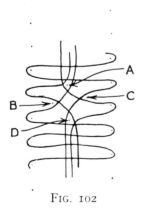

FIG. 102

It is illustrated in the Honiton sampler, Fig. 95 (5), with six holes at (6), and with five holes in the little sampler (12). For this stitch, four pinholes are needed (see enlarged braid No. 3, and Fig. 102 (3)). Bring leaders through to the middle and one pair more, then work the last but one pair passed through back through one pair. The two outside pairs of these four pairs are used as leaders; the two inner pairs are twisted three times each; put up a pin in hole *A* between them, enclose the pin with whole stitch and three twists, and leave. Work the leader pairs out to the edges, make the pinholes, and bring back to the twisted pairs.

Twist the leaders three times each, and work them through the other twisted pairs to the middle, then twist all four pairs three times each, put up pins in the two side holes (*B* and *C*) on the *outside* of the four pairs. Work the two middle pairs together in whole stitch and three twists, put up pin in the lower hole *D* between them and leave; take the leaders out to the edge, make pinholes, enclose and bring leaders through to the middle, work them together in whole stitch. Use the pair from the opposite side to the next pinhole as the leader pair and continue the braid; the other leader pair will hang down in the middle and remain passive.

Five-, Six-, Seven-, and Eight-pin Buds.

These are made by the same method as the four-pin bud. Odd numbers are useful for helping to turn a curved braid. Arrange the pinholes so that one is in the middle at the top and one in the middle at the bottom; the extra hole or holes must, of course, be arranged on the outer side. Working the leaders to and fro as before explained gains one or more pinholes and helps to turn the curve.

Winkie Pins or "Snatch Pins."

Another variety of fancy hole is made by using twisted loops (called "winkie pins" or "snatch pins")[1] for the pinholes at the sides, instead of crossing the pairs in the way previously explained. This method is illustrated in the Honiton sampler, Fig. 95 (7).

4. *Zigzag Holes.*

(Fourteen pairs required.) Illustrated in Honiton sampler, Fig. 95 (9), and in the enlarged braids at Fig. 101 (4). Work the leaders across the braid except the last passive pair and the edge pair. Leave the leaders and take the last pair but one just passed through. Work them in whole stitch with the pair between them and the leader pair.[2] Make a whole stitch with the leaders and the pair just worked.

---

[1] Winkie or snatch pins are simply-formed loops made by twisting the leaders at the end of a row, putting up the pin and working the leaders back again, without making the usual edge stitch.

[2] *Note.* Do not work this whole stitch very tightly or it will pull the holes out of the right place.

Leave these two pairs out. Take the next pair as leaders, work out to the edge and back again to where the two pairs were left out. Leave the leaders and take the last pair but one just passed through and work as before, leaving another two pairs out. Again take the next pair as leaders to the edge and back, continuing as before until four sets of two pairs have been left out and the next pinhole covered.

OPPOSITE SIDE. Take as leaders the end pair left out from the first side. Work out to the edge and back, taking in the next pair left out from the first side. Leave these leaders and use the last pair taken in instead. Work out to the edge and back taking in the two next pairs from the first side. Leave these leaders and again use the last pair taken in instead. Continue this. When all four sets have been taken in, work the new leaders out to the edge and back, working right across, then work right across and back again, and then commence leaving out the sets of two pairs from the reverse side. The direction of the holes may vary, instead of zigzag; they look well all in the same direction.

Braid Dividing into Two (Fig. 103).

Work as usual down to the first pinhole of the division. Divide the pairs into two equal parts. Bring the leaders across to the middle

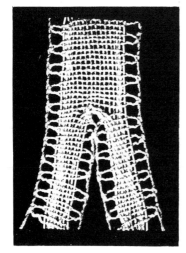

and through two more pairs; then work the last pair but one passed through back, through one pair. Put up a pin in the top hole, leaving an equal number of bobbins on both sides. If gimps are being used, hang them with one ordinary pair round the middle pin. Pass the gimp pairs out through one pair in whole stitch. Hang in two more pairs, one on each of the two middle pairs (care must be taken not to pull these new pairs tightly at first as they are not supported by pins). Work the two middle pairs together in whole stitch, twist them three times and leave to form the edge pairs for the new inner

FIG. 103

96

sides. Use the new pairs from between these and the gimp pairs each as a leader pair and continue the braid.

Gimp Threads (*Fig.* 104).

Gimp is a heavy shiny flax thread used to outline flat Honiton lace. It is not used in raised work, therefore must not be confused with the rolled outline which often occurs in the better work, and which unfortunately is known by the same name. Gimp threads are often called by the workers "Cottons." Sometimes larger bobbins are used to carry the gimp threads. When setting up, place the gimps so that they fall on the outer sides of the passives. They are woven in the usual way, each gimp being used with the next passive to form a pair.

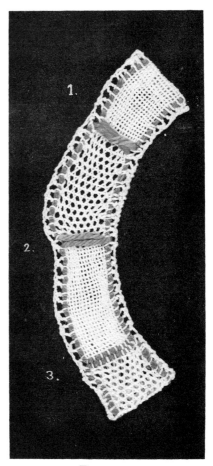

Never make a half-stitch with a gimp pair.

Pretty effects can be obtained by crossing these gimps; this crossing often marks a change of stitch (see Fig. 104). The crossing of gimps is indicated in the pricking by a single hole pricked where the gimp threads are to cross.

When working half-stitch edged with gimps, the leaders work one whole stitch with the gimp pair, then twist the leader pair once before travelling across in half-stitch.

FIG. 104

Crossing Gimps. First Method. No. 1 (*Fig.* 104).

When the leaders are at the edge, take the gimps one in each hand and, using the tails of the bobbins, pass them both under all the other passives, so that they change places. Continue working, but do not pull the gimps too tightly.

Second Method. No. 2 (Fig. 104).

When the leaders are at the edge, pass the gimp from the outer edge under all the passives, twist it once round the inner gimp, then pass it back again under the passives to the outer edge. Keep the inner gimp pulled quite tightly, and continue the weaving.

Third Method. No. 3 (Fig. 104).

When the leaders are at the edge, weave the outside gimp across, over and under the passives, alternating the movement with that of the last leader. Pass the gimp round the inside gimp and weave it back again to the outside.

Two gimps can be woven across one after the other, so that they change places as in the first method.

If the space to be crossed is wide it is better to weave the gimps across.

Curved Braids and Corners.

A curved braid is woven in the same way as a straight one, the pinholes on the inner side being placed a little closer together. When making the pricking, first space off those on the outer edge, then carefully prick the inner holes so that they alternate with those of the first side. The holes must not be too close together or the work will become clumsy.

When the curve is too sharp to allow of the same number of holes being pricked on both sides, a blind pin is made by which one pinhole on the inner side is used to serve the purpose of two.

To Work a Blind Pin.

Bring the leaders from the outer edge through all the passives to the inside, but do not make the usual edge stitch. Leave the edge pair unworked. Put up the pin, then bring the leaders round it, twisting them once. Work the leaders back again to the outer edge; make the usual pinhole. Bring the leaders back to the inner side, through all the passives, then take out the last pin (called the blind pin) and put it back into the same hole, not through the little twisted loop, but so that the leaders pass behind it. Now, work the leaders with the edge pair (not worked in last row), making usual twists, and continue the braid.

The same blind pin can be used more than once, but the result is often clumsy. A better way is by gaining on a pin. This method can be used instead of the blind pin or alternately with it.

Gaining on a Pin.

Bring the workers through the passives to the inner edge, leave the workers untwisted, and with the last pair of passives just passed tie one knot (to keep the other leaders up into position), then, using the knotted pair as leaders, work out to the edge and back again to the inside edge, working also through the old leaders which now form passives. Make the edge stitch as usual and continue the braid.

It is sometimes better (if the design allows it) to make a plain hole when turning a sharp corner (see page 93, Fig. 101), or some other fancy stitch can often be arranged so that it gains one or more pinholes (see "5-pin bud" in small Honiton sampler, Fig. 99).

The method describing how to turn a stem which terminates in a round form (page 104) can be applied with good results to sharp corners. (See small Honiton sampler (No. 1).)

Picots and Purl Edge.

The picots or little loops used in Honiton lace are described in the General Notes (page 26). The double picot is necessary on account of the fineness of Honiton thread.

These picots are called by the Devonshire workers "Purl pins." Those on the outer edges differ a little to the others which occur in fillings and on purl pin bars.

Along the entire edge of a piece of Honiton lace, the purl pins should form an unbroken line outside the ordinary outline. As this edging takes up a little more room in working than the usual pinhole, it must be allowed for when making the pricking, otherwise, if part of a leaf forms an outside edge, that leaf outline would become distorted, and, owing to the picot taking too much room, the other threads would be pushed out of place.

To Work the Edge Picot. Bring the leaders out to the edge, twist them three times, and work a whole stitch with the edge pair, twist outside pair seven times and make the double picot, then make a whole stitch with the next pair, twist these pairs three times each and continue the weaving.

When making a picot edging, the same leaders are always used for every row of weaving.

The picots for fillings and purl pin bars are made without the previous three twists which form a pinhole. When the last whole-stitch is made, twist the outside pair seven times and make the double picot as before, working the whole stitch after it, and continuing without further twists.

To Add and Take Out Bobbins.

It is often necessary to add or remove bobbins while the work is in progress.

To Add Bobbins. At the end of a row and before putting up the pin, hang the new pair over the twisted workers, working on as before. When using a gimp outlining, the gimp thread must be passed between the new pair, so that it remains at the edge.

It is occasionally necessary to make a whole stitch with the new pair and the pair of passives next before weaving the next row, in order to keep the new pair in position. When working a narrow pointed leaf, commence with quite a few bobbins and add pairs at once, first one side, then the other.

Never add more than one pair of bobbins at a time.

When working a curve, add bobbins on the outer side rather than on the inner.

To Take out Bobbins. Ordinary passives and gimps in cloth-work are just thrown back, afterwards being cut off. As passives are only removed because the cloth is too thick, the tiny ends will not unravel.

Always take out from the inner side of a curve rather than from the outer, and never take out the end pair of passives. If many pairs of passives are to be taken out, throw them back from different places; for instance, the second pair of one row, then the fourth or fifth of the next row, and so on.

To Tie Out.

When at the end of a part, throw out the gimps, and tie the workers round all the other threads, making two or three knots. Tie each pair together in two knots to prevent them from slipping, and pass the workers round them, one above and one under, then tie workers together in two or three knots and cut off.

Setting Up and Getting Rid of Knots.

When setting up, commence at the part that will enable the work to be carried on as far as possible without cutting off.

Arrange so that your edge pairs and the workers are without knots for sufficient length to complete one part, as knots in these threads are tiresome to manage. If, however, a break occurs, contrive to exchange the broken or knotted thread with a passive so that the broken thread can be hung round a pin.

Passive threads must have their knots (if any) arranged so that they hang in different places.

To Get Rid of Knots.

When nearing the knot of a passive thread, lift the thread with the needle pin and place it round a pin so that the knot comes up over the worked lace, let the thread hang in the same place, and continue working. The loop thus formed can be cut off later and the ends arranged with the needlepin so that they do not show. This refers only to cloth stitch. For removing a knot in half-stitch, the knotted thread must be securely tied to the end thread when at the end of a row, then hung round a pin as for whole stitch and tied again before continuing to work; the loop can be afterwards cut off. It is better and mostly possible to avoid a knot in half-stitch.

Sewings.

TAKING A SEWING. This is the method used to join lace, or parts of lace, together on the pillow while it is being worked.

To Take an Ordinary Sewing. Bring the workers through to where the join is required and twist them once. See that the part to be joined is securely pinned into position. Remove the pin from the pinhole where the join is to be made, insert the needlepin into this pinhole, and draw one of the worker threads through so as to form a loop. Pass the other worker through this loop (see illustration

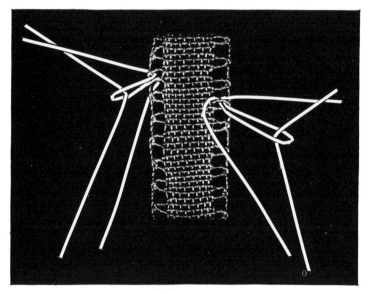

FIG. 105

on the left-hand side of Fig. 105), pull both threads carefully into position. Replace the pin to keep it firm and continue the work.

To Take a Top Sewing. This, as its name implies, is taken on the top of a finished edge. Bring the workers through to where the join is required, and twist them once. See that the part to be joined is securely pinned into place. Remove the pin from the pinhole where the join is to be made, and raise the pins on each side of it a little, but do not take them quite out. Insert the needlepin into the pinhole so as to draw one of the leaders through sideways, from under the little twisted bar formed by the workers when making the pinhole that is now being used (see illustration on the right-hand side of Fig. 105). This draws the join up more closely than an ordinary sewing and also leaves the outline free. Top sewings are necessary for all raised work, also very useful for ending off some parts.

DOUBLE SEWINGS. Occasionally, both leaders are drawn through the pinhole and two other threads passed through the double loop thus formed. It is useful when ending off where greater strength is needed.

Double sewings are often used when sewing in a number of bobbins for a filling.

When taking sewings, note that the same workers are always used for the return weaving.

On no account may sewings be taken into the holes formed only by the edge pair.

When sewing with a half-stitch leader pair, always draw the leader thread through to form the loop.

A fine crochet hook is sometimes used to take sewings, but this is not advisable, as it often strains the pinhole. The best workers never use one. A sewing needle, size 8, driven into a handle, leaving quite 1 in. of the needle free, is the right thing to use, and it is surprising how quickly one becomes used to it.

Turning Stitch and Ten-stick.

Turning stitch consists of a whole stitch and a half-stitch. (2 over 3. 2 and 4 over 1 and 3. 2 over 3. 2 and 4 over 1 and 3. 2 over 3). The end pair is then left and the next pair weave back as leaders. It sometimes improves this stitch to twist the end pair once before working the turning stitch. It is used at the edge of a braid where no pinholes are required. The extra half-stitch at the end gives firmness and enables the braid to be pulled, and held into position. This is owing to the half-stitch changing one of the leaders.

Ten-stick or Stem stitch.

This is a tiny braid with pinholes only on one side. It is usually made with five pairs, hence its name "ten-stick." It is used for stems, tiny circles, and all narrow parts which turn quickly; it also forms the little raised edge for much of the raised work.

TO WORK TEN-STICK. Hang five pairs on a pin or sew them into part of the finished lace; take an outside pair as leaders, work through to the other side, making the usual pinhole and putting up the pin. Bring the leaders back again through two passive pairs, then make a turning stitch with the last passive pair, leave the end pair and work back with the next pair making the next pinhole, and on the other side the turning stitch.

A Scroll Terminating in a Round Form (Figs. 106 and 107).

Commence with six pairs at A, working across and across as usual, and immediately increasing the number of bobbins (only five more

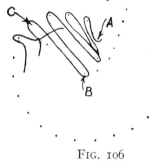

FIG. 106

pairs were added for the diagram, but the number must vary according to the curve, size of thread, etc.). One blind pin will be necessary. When arriving at C, bring the leaders across from the outside towards B, but only work through three pairs of passives. Let the leaders drop and take the third pair of passives (the last pair passed through) as leaders, work out to the edge, make edge stitch, enclose pin and leave; these leaders now hang as passives. Take out the next pair not worked in last row to the edge, put up the pin, enclose and leave this pair also. Again, take the next unworked passive pair as leaders out to the edge as before, continuing until all the unworked passives have been taken to the edge. Then proceed as for an ordinary braid. One or two sewings may be taken into hole B if necessary to help turn, also make blind pins, and gain on a pin, to keep the leaders working at the right angle.

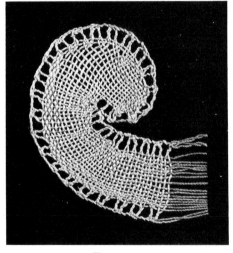

FIG. 107

104

This method of turning may be used with advantage when turning sharp corners. (See the points of the leaves in the small Honiton sampler, page 91.)

No. 1. *Honiton Leaves.*

Illustrated in the Honiton sampler, Fig. 95, at 13.

The vein is formed by the fancy braid stitch called "Mittens";

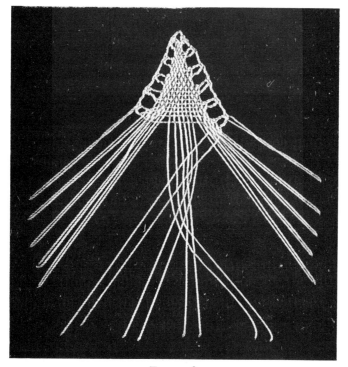

FIG. 108

a somewhat similar effect can be obtained by simply twisting the leaders each time they cross the middle of the leaf.

No. 2. Illustrated in the Honiton sampler, Fig. 95, at 10.

This leaf has whole stitch on one half, and half-stitch on the other. They are joined by sewings which form the vein.

THE PRICKING has the usual holes along the edge and a row of holes along the centre vein ending a little way from the top.

TO WORK THE LEAF. Commence at the foot and work one side

in whole stitch in the same way as a braid. When nearing the last pinhole on the inside, commence to turn and continue turning until the leader direction has turned right round. At the middle of the top change from whole to half-stitch. Work down the second side, taking sewings into the pinholes of the vein.

No. 3. Illustrated in the Honiton sampler, Fig. 95, at 14.

This leaf is of whole and half-stitch, having a vein of leadworks and winkie pins (see page 84) alternating.

THE PRICKING requires holes along the edge, and a double row of holes down the middle. These holes must be wide enough to allow of the leadwork being made between them; they must also be opposite each other, but alternating with the edge holes.

TO WORK THE LEAF. Commence at the top with whole stitch, adding bobbins as it widens. At the top of the vein leave the leaders at the edge and divide the pair in the middle. (Refer to Fig. 108, page 105.) Bring the leaders to the middle and through one pair more. Work the last pair but one passed through, back in whole stitch through one pair. These two pairs just worked together divide the leaf, and form the outside passives for the inner edges of the leaf. The old leaders continue to work across one side of the leaf, which should now be changed from whole to half-stitch. The passives hanging from between the old leaders, and the two middle pairs crossed in whole stitch, are used as leaders and worked out as leaders for the other side of the leaf. At the two top pinholes, winkie pins are made, that is, the leaders just twist three times and pass round the pin, there not being an edge pair. At the next pinhole, the leaders unite to form a leadwork. Continue these alternately for the space required then close the leaf (using all whole stitch) as follows. After the edge pinholes are worked and the leaders brought back to the middle. Bring one leader through one pair more. Make a whole stitch with the two inside edge passives, and continue working with the other leader.

Raised Honiton Lace.

The student should not attempt Raised Honiton until she has had considerable practice at the flat methods.

Raised Honiton is that kind of work, which is outlined, or partly outlined, by a little raised line. This line is sometimes made of "ten-stick," often called gimp, although it does not resemble the shiny outline of flat work. At other times, the raised line consists of a twist or roll of threads.

I am describing three leaves and one flower petal worked by raised methods. From these instructions, the worker should be able to adapt the principle to her own designs. In each instance, an enlarged pricking is given and finished work is shown in the sampler.

No. 4. *Raised Leaf Divided into Little Sections Called "Taps."*

No. 11 in Honiton sampler, Fig. 95 and Fig. 109.

Commence at *A*, and work the little "ten-stick" line down the middle to *B*. All pins must be pushed well down and raised one at a time when necessary for sewings. From *B* hang in two pairs at each hole up to *C*. To hang in these pairs, one is hung over the leaders before working the edge pinhole, the other is hung over the leaders after making the edge pinhole. Lay the new pairs carefully aside (over the "ten-stick") in order, as they are hung up; this is most important. When the pin is put up at *C*, work back through three passive pairs and also through four or six of those just hung in; then, in order to keep the work well up in place, tie up with the last passive pair worked through. Use the tied pair as leaders, work out to the edge and back, taking in two or three more pairs; tie up again as before, work to edge and back again through all the pairs and tying up. Continue working across. When

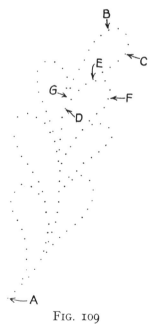

FIG. 109

at the gimp side, top sewings (see page 102) must be taken to connect to the gimp, cut out pairs as the leaf gets narrower. When the pin is put up at *D*, work to the middle, take the top sewing, and work out to the edge, twist the leaders once before working through the outside pair, tie the leaders twice, and work back with the next pair; take a *double* top sewing when at the gimp side, tie the pairs twice and tie all between, cut off the pairs so that only six are left, leave one of these pairs hanging, and take another pair, twist it round and round the other four pairs, making a roll long enough to reach to *E*, and leave. Use the pair left out at the base to take sewings into every other pinhole; these sewings must be taken so that one thread passes over and the other thread under the roll so as to fasten the roll to the pinholes. At pinhole *E* work gimp along edge to *F*, putting in pairs as before, continue until all four little "taps" are finished on one side of the leaf, then cut off and commence again at *G*, by hanging in five fresh pairs.

No. 5. *Leaf with Serrations.*

The middle of this leaf has a double row of " ten-stick " united by a ladder of leadworks. (See Honiton sampler, Fig. 95 (12) and Fig. 110.)

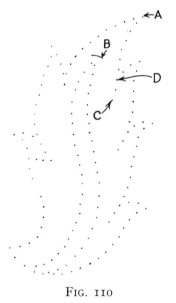

FIG. 110

THE PRICKING requires holes along the edges, and a double row of holes down the middle. These holes must be wide enough apart to allow the clothing of the "ten-stick" and the leadworks to come between; prick these holes opposite each other.

TO WORK THE LEAF. Commence at the foot of the vein, make the "ten-stick" to the top of the vein, and when returning along the other side make the cutworks at every other pinhole. For this, one pair must be sewn in to the pinhole opposite the top leadwork, the sewing being taken over and under the "ten-stick" cloth as if it were a rolled edge. The new pair is used with the leader of the opposite "ten-stick" to make the leadwork, it is again sewn to the "ten-stick," twisted two or three times, and sewn a little lower ready for the next leadwork. When centre vein is finished, tie out and cut off.

Set up at *A*, work the top of the leaf as usual down to *B*. After the leaders have passed through half the pairs, take a sewing with the leaders into the top pinhole of the vein. Divide the pairs into two, and leave one half to work the left side. Work the right side down to the last pinhole at *C*. Hang in a new pair behind the pin, work through six pairs, make a turning stitch, and roll back the six pairs up to *D*. From *D* work " ten-stick," hanging in new pairs as required up to the point. Work across and across, tying up to the new pairs as explained in the first raised leaf, and taking sewings down to pinhole *C*, then work right across to the middle. The remainder of the leaf is simply a repetition of this, with any slight alteration the outline may require.

No. 6. *Leaf with Veins Raised on Half-stitch.*

This leaf is illustrated in the Honiton sampler, Fig. 95 (15) and Fig. III). The raised vein is worked first.

Commence at *A*. Make a " ten-stick " gimp with six pairs (instead of the usual five) down to *B*, putting up the pins on the left side. At *B* the pairs are divided. To do this, *after* working the leaders through the passives, do not work the edge stitch, nor put up the pin, but put the edge pair under three pairs, leave these (the edge pair) and two passive pairs to work the vein on the right-hand side.

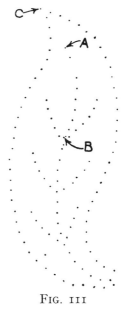

FIG. III

Now work the vein on the left side with the three left-hand pairs. Use the two right-hand pairs and make a turning stitch. With the two left-hand pairs make the usual edge stitch, put up the pin at *B*, then repeat the turning stitch with the two right-hand pairs, and also the edge stitch and pin; continue thus until the top pin is put up, work out through the edge pair and tie up with leader pair. Make a whole stitch with the two left-hand pairs; put the right-hand pair between them and "double tie" once (that is, tying with two double threads). Roll the right-hand pair over the others twice;

sew into the next pinhole, roll twice again, and sew into the next but one pinhole, and so on. Always sew into the bottom pinhole and tie between the leaders.

Find the old edge pair which was passed under and left for the other side, pass them back under the three pairs just worked, leave them. With the last pair but one from the right side, work through three pairs and tie them up twice.

Make the vein on the right-hand side with the three right-hand pairs. When the veins are complete, work the half-stitch leaf over them. Hang pairs at *C*, work half-stitch, adding pairs as required until you come to *A*, where the pairs are divided, the leaf now being worked in two parts. Take a sewing into the top of vein at *A*. All sewings must be taken with the worker thread forming the loop. Continue the half-stitch down one side, sewing into every pinhole down the centre vein, also sew into each tip and about every other hole of the side veins. The other side is, of course, worked in the same way.

Flower Petal.

These flowers have a raised circle with a leadwork in the middle, the petals mostly raised and so arranged that the bobbins do not all have to be cut off each time (see Fig. 112).

It is illustrated in the Honiton sampler, Fig. 95 (11A). First work the centre circle in " ten-stick," using six pairs instead of the usual

Fig. 112

five. Join it by a double sewing and tie all between. Work the " ten-stick " gimp from *A* to *B* and hang in two pairs at each of the next four holes, as described in the raised Honiton leaf, No. 4, page 107. Continue working and tie up with the new pairs and then by top-sewings. When at the bottom, work half-way across, leaving six pairs not worked, sew the leaders to the circle, work whole stitch back through one pair, tie both these pairs and cut off. Sew the next pair to the circle, make whole stitch as before, tie and cut off, repeat twice more. There should be only the six pairs left to finish the other part of the petal. Take the pair next to middle which was not worked in the last row, sew into the circle, put back the pin, enclose it with a whole stitch worked with the next pair, and leave. Again, take the next pair not worked, work it through two pairs, sew into the circle and, enclosing pin as before, leave. Now take a double sewing, tie all six pairs between and roll up to *B*, in the next petal, continue as before.

Honiton Backgrounds.

There are three kinds of pillow-made grounding used in Honiton lace.

First.

No. 16 in the Honiton sampler, Fig. 95. Purl-pin bars are arranged to form an open network. These bars consist of a plait of three or four pairs; upon one side of the plait picots are worked at intervals.

The lines of this groundwork should always be drawn in upon the working drawing, and travel to and from points *between* two pin-holes of the edges to be joined. This grounding must be arranged to give a uniform appearance to the whole piece of lace. Strength and simplicity must be aimed at. Avoid lines running at various angles, but at the same time, take care to prevent unnecessary hanging-in of threads.

The Pricking. The holes for the picot pins should be pricked on the right-hand side of the bar line, and at equal distances of not more than one-twelfth of an inch apart.

To Work the Bar. Hang (by "sewings") four pairs to the two pinholes at the commencing point. Take one of the edge pairs, work it through to the other side, twist it once and leave it. Work back with the last pair passed through, twist this also once and leave it. Again take the last pair passed through out to the other side as before. This continued should result in a tightly-plaited flat braid.

When arriving at a pinhole, twist the leader pair seven times and make a double picot (explained in the General Notes, page 26), and work back with the same pair as leaders.

To join the bar to the next part of the design, make a sewing with the leader pair into the top pinhole of the two, where the join is to be made; then work the next pair through it in whole stitch, and with this pair take another sewing into the second of the two pinholes. This not only strengthens the connection, but keeps the little plait quite flat.

When two purl-pin bars cross, they should both be worked to the crossing point, then the pairs all crossed in whole stitch, using two threads together as one.

A plait of three pairs is worked by the same method, and in most cases it is preferable to the thicker plait.

Second. "Trolly Net."

Known in the Midlands as point ground. It is illustrated in the Honiton sampler, Fig. 95, at 18. In the next part of this book on "Bucks Point," it is fully explained, and there is an enlarged working diagram on page 151.

In Honiton lace, the edge braid called "foot side" is not required, the net being worked into the spaces in the same way as a "filling." With practice it is possible to put in this net without a pricking, but not advisable to a beginner.

THE PRICKING is made upon parallel lines crossing other parallel lines at an angle; 62 degrees is useful for Honiton grounding, and 14 or 16 to the inch is not too close. For explanation of angles, see page 145.

It is necessary that all the lines of the net should run in the same direction throughout the piece of lace.

To WORK THE NET. The pairs must be sewn into the edge pinholes so that one pair hangs between each pinhole and the next of a line of holes in the pricking. At the right-hand side one pair is sewn in as leaders, just above the line of pinholes to be used. Twist each pair three times. Work in slanting rows downwards from right to left. With the leaders and the next pair on the left make a half-stitch and two extra twists. Put up a pin between the pairs, but do not enclose; drop the right-hand pair and work the stitch with the leaders and the next pair on their left. Put up next pin. Continue to end of row, sew into the edge pinhole. If the space widens, the leaders are not tied and cut out, but left twisted, and hang down beside the others. Pairs must be added or cut out as space requires.

NOTE. A heavier make of bobbin is better than the usual Honiton "stick" for this grounding.

Third. Point d'Angleterre Net (Fig. 113).

This net is illustrated in the Honiton sampler, Fig. 95, at 17, also accompanying enlarged diagram. It is worked without a pricking, in rows across and across horizontally. Like other groundings, the rows of meshes must all run in the same direction.

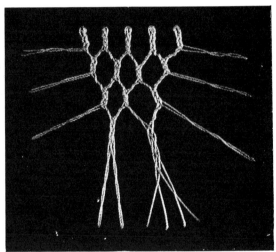

To Work the Net. Sew in two pairs together at intervals of about one-sixteenth of an inch along the top line. With each set of four threads, make a plait or bar of four half-stitches, then twist each pair three times, and leave. The next row is worked in the same way, but using a

FIG. 113

pair from one plait with a pair from the next plait in order to work the under plait so that the rows of plaits alternate. Of course, pairs must be added or taken out according to the shape to be grounded.

Honiton Fillings.

These are the fancy stitches which occur in various spaces, sometimes enclosed by parts of a design, and sometimes within the design as the centre of a flower, leaf, etc.

Do not allow the fillings to become confused with the background which must be kept distinct from the ornament upon it.

Great care is necessary to decide the fillings, and they must also be set in at the correct angle. Do not be tempted to "hang in" at the narrowest part of the space just because it often happens to be easier to work that way. The little trouble spent in roughly sketching in fillings on your working drawing is well repaid by the result. It is much less trouble to rub out and re-arrange on a drawing what, if worked, would take many hours to unpick, or cut out, and rework, besides risking a broken or weakened edge. The drawing will serve as a guide to spacing the spots or heavier parts as well as the angle and general appearance of it.

When arranging a filling, design it if possible to fit the space. A filling may radiate or be based upon curved lines, if the design is improved by it.

In describing the fillings, I have given the directions for working one repeat as if worked from a horizontal line, and the pairs are just hung from a row of pins. The enlarged worked diagram shows a portion finished, also a repeat unfinished and left loose to show the working more clearly. It should not be difficult for a worker to commence at any part of the filling required by the design.

To Work in a Filling.

The bobbins must be wound in pairs (see page 11), and have sufficient thread without a knot to complete the filling.

Hang in the pairs by means of sewings taken into the pin-holes at the edge of the space to be filled; occasionally a pair must be hung in between two pinholes, but avoid this if possible.

Replace all edge pins and push them well down.

Work the filling in rows horizontally or obliquely as the directions explain, adding more pairs or tying some out as the shape requires. Tied pairs are better put back to cut off later, as, if a mistake is discovered, it gives a chance of altering it.

When the filling is finished, take sewings into the other edge pin-holes, tie each pair three times (see page 13), and cut off. Remove pins after the bobbins are cut off.

When sewing out the leader pair from a cutwork, always draw the passive thread through the edge hole to form the loop for the leader thread to pass through. This prevents the cutwork from drawing up.

Filling. The Cutwork or Leadwork.

The little plaits used in Honiton lace are called cutworks or lead-works, according to the locality in which they are made. They play a very important part in this lace, more especially in the fillings. One is often used alone, in the centre of a flower (see Honiton sampler, Fig. 95, space 19).

When six are clustered in a round space as in the same sampler at (34), it is called a "cartwheel." The method of crossing these in the middle so as to form a hole is explained in the General Methods (page 28). The cutworks are sometimes square, sometimes oblong, but the method of working is always the same; it is fully explained in the General Notes, on page 22.

Cutwork with Hole.

A pretty variety can be made by twisting the pairs in the middle of the cutwork so as to form a hole; this more frequently occurs in old than in modern Honiton, where also many pretty arrangements of cutworks can be seen used for centering flowers.

Honiton Diamond Filling (Figs. 114 and 115).

This filling takes its name from the direction of the leadworks and crossings.

It is to be seen in the Victoria and Albert Museum, Lace, No. T19—1911. The illustration in the Honiton sampler, Fig. 95, space 20, was worked with No. 12 S. thread.

THE PRICKING was made in sets of four holes, these sets being arranged diagonally, the distance from the centre of one set to the centre of the next measured horizontally, being one-sixth of an inch, and each little square or set of holes about one twenty-fourth of an inch.

TO WORK THE FILLING. Hang up two pairs at each pin-hole A and B, twisting each three times. With the two pairs from A, make a leadwork to E, twist each three times, put up a pin between them, and leave. With the two pairs from B, make another leadwork to F, twisting three times and putting up pin as before, leave. Cross these four pairs as follows: whole stitch with two centre pairs, twist

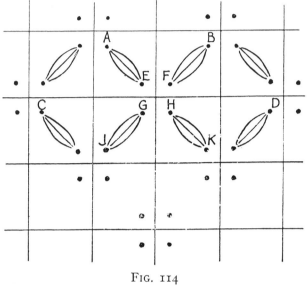

FIG. 114

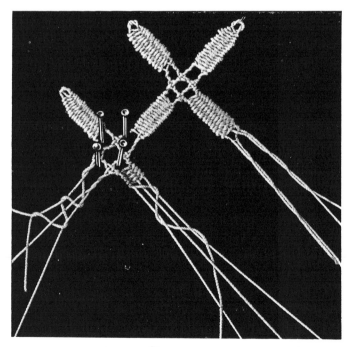

FIG. 115

three times. Whole stitch with two left-hand pairs, twist three times, put up a pin between them in hole *G*, leave. Whole stitch with two right-hand pairs, twist three times, put up a pin between them in hole *H*, leave. Whole stitch with the two centre pairs, twist three times, leave. The last

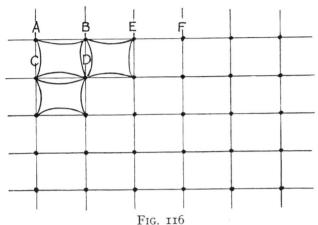

two pins put up are enclosed by lead-works being made with each two pairs from these pins. The leadwork from *G* works down to *I*, and that from *H* works down to *K*, where they will cross others in a similar way.

FIG. 116

Honiton "Brick" Filling (Figs. 116 and 117).

This filling consists of rows of square leadworks and pin-holes.

It is to be seen in the Victoria and Albert Museum, Lace, No. 570—1905. The illustration in the Honiton sampler, Fig. 95, space 21, was worked with No. 12 S. thread, and pricked upon lines twenty to the inch vertically, and 16 to the inch horizontally.

To WORK THE FILLING. Hang up two pairs at each of the four top pinholes, and enclose the pins with whole stitch and one twist.

With the second and

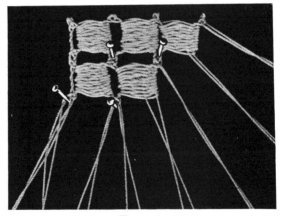

FIG. 117

third pairs make a leadwork down to the next row of holes. Now with the leader pair and the next pair to the left (which in the case of a "filling" is sewn into the braid, but here just twisted from the upper hole) make a whole stitch and one twist, put up a pin in the lower hole on the left, enclose it with whole stitch and one twist, leave.

Make a similar lead-work with the fourth and fifth pairs, with this leader pair and the next to the left (which hangs from the first leadwork) make a whole stitch, and one twist, put up pin in hole under it, enclose with whole stitch and one twist. Continue to end of row. Each row is the same.

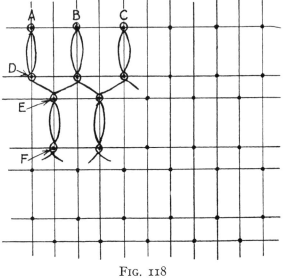

FIG. 118

Honiton Pin Filling (*Figs*. 118 *and* 119).

This filling consists of rows of long leadworks, each having a pinhole at the top and bottom.

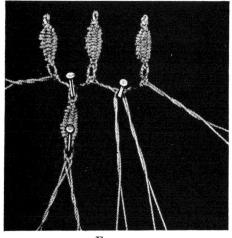

FIG. 119

The leadworks of one row alternate with those of the next.

It can be seen in the Victoria and Albert Museum, Lace, No. 785—64. The illustration in the Honiton sampler, Fig. 95, space 22, was worked with No. 12 S. thread.

THE PRICKING was made so that the leadworks were one-sixteenth of an inch apart. The distance from the top pinhole to the one at the bottom of the leadwork is also one-sixteenth of an inch. As the rows of leadworks alternate, the pricking for every other row was marked out first, leaving one-eighth of an inch between in which the alternate leadworks were fitted.

To Work the Filling. Hang up two pairs at each pinhole, A, B, and C, enclose the pins with three twists, whole stitch, and one twist.

With two pairs from A, make a leadwork down to the pinhole D, put up a pin between these two pairs, twist each three times and enclose pin with whole stitch and three twists. Do the same with the next two pairs from B, enclosing lower pin as before. Now take the second and third pairs (one pair from each leadwork just finished), make a whole stitch, put up a pin in E, enclose with whole stitch and one twist, and make a leadwork down to the lower pinhole F, twist and enclose as before. It is better to complete each row across the filling before commencing the next.

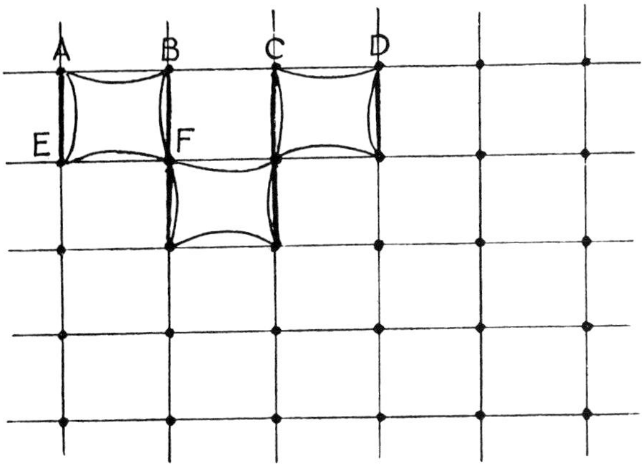

Fig. 120

Honiton "Cushion" Filling (Figs. 120 and 121).

This filling consists of rather shallow leadworks, and pinholes at the corners of each. The leadworks are arranged in horizontal rows, and those of one row alternate with those in the rows above and under them.

It can be seen in the Victoria and Albert Museum, Lace, No. 570—1909. The illustration in the Honiton sampler, Fig. 95, space 23, was worked with No. 12 S. thread.

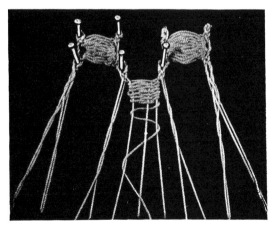

Fig. 121

The Pricking was made in horizontal rows one-twentieth of an inch apart, and vertical rows one-sixteenth of an inch apart.

To Work the Filling. Hang up two pairs at *A*, *B*, *C*, and *D*, twist each three times and enclose the pins with whole stitch. Of the first four pairs, twist the two outer pairs three times and leave. Twist the two inner pairs once and make a leadwork down to *E* and *F*, twist the right-hand pair once, make a whole stitch with it and the twisted left-hand pair from *B*, put up pin in *F*, twist pairs three times, and enclose with whole stitch. Twist the right-hand pair once and the left-hand pair three times, leave. With the left-hand pair from the leadwork and the twisted pair left from *A*, make a whole stitch, twist each pair three times, put up a pin in *E*, enclose with whole stitch, twist the right-hand pair three times and the left-hand pair once, and leave. Make another leadwork with the inner pairs from *C* and *D*, enclosing lower pins as before, continue until top line of leadworks is finished. The next row is worked in the same way, but making a leadwork come under the space of the row above.

Honiton "No-pin" Filling (Figs. 122 and 123).

This filling, as its name implies, is made without pins, and consists of rows of square leadworks and spaces, each row alternating with that above and below it.

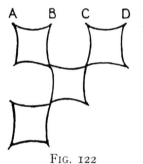

FIG. 122

It can be seen in the Victoria and Albert Museum, Lace, No. T19—1911.

The illustration in the Honiton sampler, Fig. 95, space 24, was worked with No. 12 S. thread.

The leadworks are about one sixteenth of an inch square.

It is worked diagonally, in rows from the right hand down to the left, commencing at the top left-hand corner.

The same leader must be used for all the leadworks in one row.[1]

To Work the Filling. Hang into the top edge of space *A*, *B*, *C*, *D*, etc., single pairs at intervals of one-sixteenth of an inch apart, and leave each pair twisted once. With the first two pairs from the left side (from *A* and *B*) make a square leadwork, twisting each pair once. The left-hand or leader pair should be sewn out into the edge

[1] To prevent them from drawing up.

120

of filling. Make a second leadwork with the two next pairs (from *C* and *D*), twist each pair once. The leader should always end as the second bobbin, so that the one twist will take it over the first passive, then it should at once commence the next leadwork, which is made with the leader pair from first leadwork and the right-hand pair from the other leadwork. After the leader makes the extra twist it travels or weaves to the left under the second and over the first passive

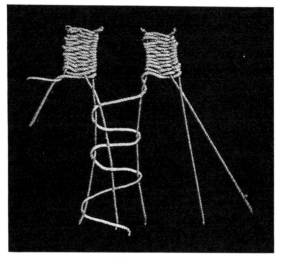

FIG. 123

of the new leadwork. This is clearly shown in the working diagram. Continue as before.

Honiton "Toad-in-the-hole" Filling (Figs. 124 and 125).

This filling consists of cloth-stitch bars called "walls" between which are square leadworks called "toads." The rows are alternate, so that the leadworks of one row are immediately under and over the cloth-stitch bars of the rows above and below them. It can be seen in the Victoria and Albert Museum, Lace, T19—1911, in a wide lace of the early nineteenth century.

The illustration in the Honiton sampler, Fig. 95, space 25, was worked with No. 12 S. thread.

THE PRICKING was made so that the whole-stitch bars of six holes are one-sixteenth of an inch wide and one-twelfth of an inch deep, one-eighth of an inch being left between each group of six holes. From the top of one group to the top of the group immediately under it is one-quarter of an inch. Every other row was marked out first, the space being left for the alternate rows to be put in after.

To Work the Filling. Hang up two pairs just above *A*, and

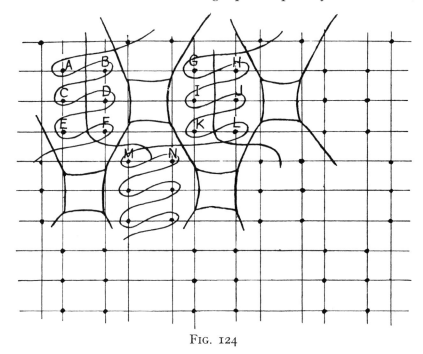

FIG. 124

make a whole stitch. Hang three pairs just above *B*. Take the first of these three pairs through the other two in whole stitch, twist three times, and leave them for the leadwork. Use the last pair passed through as leaders, work through three pairs to the left in whole stitch, twist three times, put up a pin in hole *A* between the leaders and passives, bring the leaders back through the three passives to *B*, put up pin and twist as before, continuing until pin *F* is put up. Do not twist leaders, but cover pin with a whole stitch, leave these, make a whole stitch with the other two passives, leaving them also.

Hang up three pairs just above *G* and three other pairs just above *H*. Work out the two inner pairs in whole stitch, through the two outer pairs.

The inner pairs are to be used later for the leadworks.

Make the next whole-stitch bar with the four centre pairs of those hung up last, using the right-hand pair as leaders. When this bar is finished, leave. Use the two twisted pairs hanging between the two bars, make a square leadwork, then twist each of the two pairs

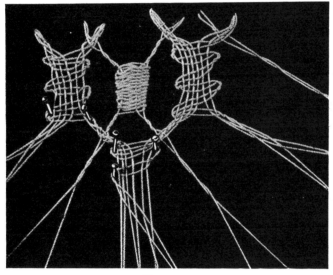

FIG. 125

three times. Work out the left pair to the left in whole stitch through the two pairs hanging from the first whole-stitch bar, twist three times and leave for another leadwork. Work out the right-hand pair from the leadwork to the right in whole stitch through the two pairs hanging from the second whole-stitch bar, twist three times and leave for another leadwork. With the four pairs now between the twisted pairs from the leadwork, make another whole-stitch bar under this leadwork. It is better to complete one row across the filling before commencing the next.

Honiton "Blossom" Filling (*Fig.* 126).

This is a similar filling to the "Toad-in-the-hole," consisting as it does of little whole-stitch blocks and square leadworks alternating.

The illustration in the Honiton sampler, Fig. 95, space 26, was worked with No. 12 S. thread.

THE PRICKING was made in sets of four holes, these sets being pricked and arranged diagonally. The distance from the centre of one set of holes to the centre of the next set diagonally is one-sixth

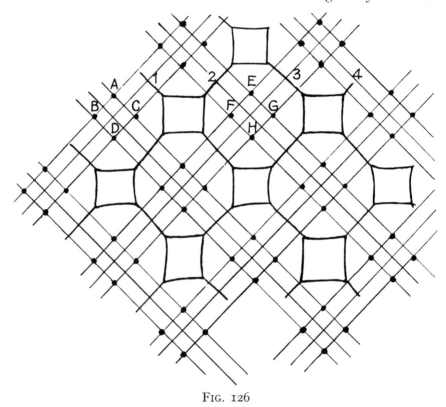

FIG. 126

of an inch, and each little group of holes forms a square one twenty-fourth of an inch.

It is worked in rows horizontally, a whole-stitch block, and then a leadwork, but it is better to finish one row before the next is commenced.

TO WORK THE FILLING. For the first whole-stitch block, hang up four pairs at *A*, enclose the pin by using the right-hand pair as leaders, work them across to the left through three pairs in whole stitch, put up pin in hole *B* between the leaders and end passives, twist leaders three times and bring them back in whole stitch, through to hole *C*, put up pin, twist as before, and work back to other side; put up pin in *D*, as before twist leaders and work back again through two pairs. Now, with these leaders and end pair, make a half-stitch plait of four half-stitches, and leave.

NOTE. Four half-stitches are not the same as two whole stitches; see general instructions. Hang up four pairs at *E* and make another whole-stitch block, ending with the half-stitch plaits as before.

For the leadwork, hand up two pairs at points 1 and 2, twist each three times, and make a square leadwork, leave pairs twisted three times, leaving the leader on the outer side. Now pass the leader pair in whole stitch through the two pairs from the right-hand half-stitch plait, at the foot of the first whole-stitch block. Twist three times, leave. Make another half-stitch plait with the four pairs just passed through. The right-hand pair from the leadwork is passed in whole stitch through the two pairs from the left-hand half-stitch plait of the second whole-stitch block, twist three times, leave. Make another half-stitch plait with the four just passed through. Make another leadwork with two pairs hung from points 3 and 4, taking the twisted pairs through the half-stitch plaits, leaving plaits and twists ready for next row.

For the next row make a whole-stitch block under the leadwork, using the four pairs from the half-stitch plaits above. To commence this block, take the second pair from the left as the leaders through the next two pairs, put up a pin in the top hole, twist the leaders and bring back as before, continuing as for the first block. After this, make a leadwork with the twisted pairs passed through the half-stitch plaits, from the other leadworks.

Honiton "Swing-and-a-pin" Filling (Figs. 127 and 128).

This, and the other swing fillings are named from the method of working, the leadworks being swung from point to point without the support of pins. This variety has rows of pin-holes between the leadworks, and can be seen in the Victoria and Albert Museum, Lace, No. 506—1883, in an eighteenth-century lappet.

The illustration in the Honiton sampler, Fig. 95, space 27, was worked with No. 12 S. thread. The pricking was made in rows diagonally upon sectional paper ten to the inch, making a hole at

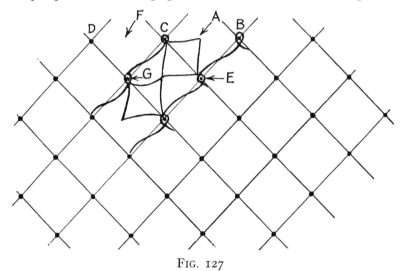

FIG. 127

every crossing and also in the middle of each square or diamond. It is worked in lines diagonally, from the right hand down towards the left, commencing at the top left-hand corner of the space to be filled.

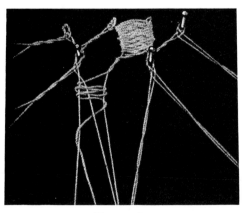

FIG. 128

To Work the Filling. Hang up two pairs each at B, C, and D, twist three times, enclose pins with whole stitch. The right-hand pair of each is twisted once and left to make a leadwork. Twist the left-hand pair of each three times and leave. Hang up one pair at point A (over hole E, and midway between B and C). Hang another pair at point F (between C and D and over hole G); twist each once, leave. Twist the pair from A once, use it with the right-hand pair from C to make a square leadwork down to G and E.

126

Twist the left-hand pair from this leadwork once and leave it ready for the next leadwork. Twist the right-hand pair once, and use it with the left-hand pair from *B* to make a whole stitch, twist each pair three times, put up the pin in between pairs at hole *E*, enclose pin with whole stitch. Twist the right-hand pair once, and the left-hand pair three times, and leave. Do the same with the left-hand pair from *D*, and the right-hand pair from *C*, twisting, putting up, and enclosing pin *G*, then twist the left-hand pair three times, and the right-hand pair once, to use for a leadwork made with the next pair hanging from the last leadwork. The same leader must be used for all the leadworks in one row, in order to prevent them from drawing up.

Point d'Esprit Fillings.

Point d'Esprit means "spotted net" in pillow lace.

There are many varieties. The spots may be evenly distributed or arranged in groups or lines.

The illustration in the small Honiton sampler, Fig. 99 (11), shows a single spotting upon Trolly net; it can also be seen in the Victoria and Albert Museum, Lace, 699—86. For working the net, see the Bucks Point part, page 151. This filling was pricked on parallel lines, one millimetre apart and angled at 60 degrees.

Space 28 in the larger Honiton sampler, Fig. 95, shows another variety with groups of four cutworks. This pricking was made upon 16 to the inch sectional paper, using every crossing for a pinhole in the network, and leaving spaces for the cutworks.[1] The method of working is so similar to the "Swing-and-a-pin" filling, page 125, that further description is not necessary. Still further varieties may be seen in the Victoria and Albert Museum, Lace, 699—86.

Pearl Filling (Figs. 129 and 130).

This filling consists of groups of four purl pins connected with each other diagonally by half-stitch plaits.

The illustration in the Honiton sampler, Fig. 95, space 29, was

[1] No 12 S. thread was used for both these fillings.

worked with 12 S. thread. It can be seen in the Victoria and Albert Museum, Lace, T22—1911. It is pricked and worked diagonally.

THE PRICKING was made so that the distance from the middle of one group of holes to the middle of the next is one-sixth of an inch, measured diagonally. Each little group of holes would form a square of one twenty-fourth of an inch.

TO WORK THE FILLING. For one repeat of this filling, use four pairs of bobbins, two hanging from *A* and two from *B* from braid

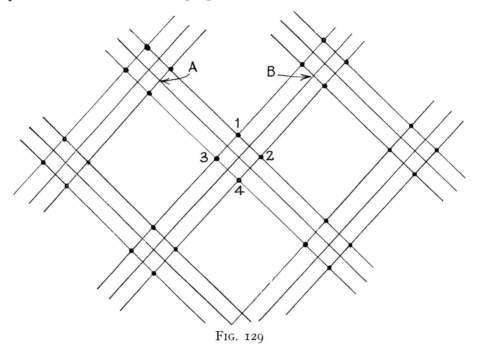

FIG. 129

edge or from *between* sets of other holes. With each two pairs make a half-stitch plait long enough to reach to the first set of four holes under them. Use the right-hand pair of the left-hand plait to make a purl pin in the top hole No. 1 (twist three or four times before putting up a pin and once after), then make a whole stitch with the two left-hand pairs.

With the two middle pairs (of the four pairs) make a whole stitch and one twist.

Work the two right-hand pairs in whole stitch and make a purl pin in hole 2, also make a whole stitch with the two right-hand pairs.

Work the two left-hand pairs in whole stitch, and make a purl pin in hole 3, also make a whole stitch with the two left-hand pairs.

Twist the two middle pairs once and make a whole stitch with them.

Work the two right-hand pairs in whole stitch and make a purl pin in hole 4, using the left of the two pairs for the purl pin, and

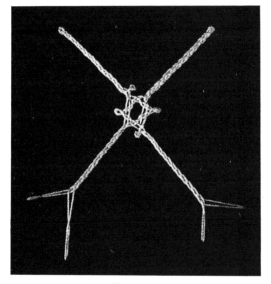

FIG. 130

working the two right-hand pairs into a half-stitch plait down to the next group of holes.

Make another half-stitch plait with the two other pairs. These plaits will meet others and are used with them for working the next purl pin groups.

Double Ground Filling.

The Double Ground filling is a repetition of the little five-hole crossing used in the diamond filling (page 115), therefore the working need not be again described. A whole stitch is worked to enclose the pin instead of making a cutwork. It is to be seen in the Victoria and Albert Museum, Lace, No. T69—1913. The illustration in the Honiton sampler, Fig. 95, space 30, was worked with No. 12 S. thread.

The pricking is similar to that used for the Diamond filling, but the little groups of holes are pricked closer together. The distance from the lowest hole of one group to the top hole of the group under it, equals that between the top and bottom holes of a group.

Double Ground with Cutworks.

A variety of the above filling.

Prick the groups of holes a *very* little farther apart. Work a cutwork in the intervening spaces.

The illustration in the Honiton sampler, Fig. 95, space 31, should be sufficient guide. It will be seen that the cutwork pairs pass through the whole stitch which encloses the pin.

Filling. Bars and Cutworks.

Bars of a very narrow braid (sometimes with the usual pin-hole edge and sometimes having only a winkie pin edge) are joined by cutworks worked in a zigzag manner. They form a very suitable filling for some spaces. They are too simple to need further illustration than reference to the Honiton sampler, Fig. 95, spaces 32 and 33. Five pairs of passives were used for these, the only difference being that the cutworks of one have a hole in the middle of each.

Instead of cutworks, little plaited bars of half-stitches can be used to connect the little braids; or two pairs may be sewn to the bars opposite each other, then twisted and crossed by means of a whole stitch, and again twisted and sewn to the opposite bars at the next pinhole in a similar manner to the leaders in the fancy braid stitch called "mittens."

Another variety has the cutworks placed squarely between the bars in a similar manner to one of the Bucks Point fillings.

Bars need not run parallel, but sometimes cross each other, leaving a square space in which a cutwork is placed. This filling is too course for most Honiton lace.

Filling. Hexagonal Bride.

This filling consists of half-stitch plaits or bars with double picots. The bars are arranged so as to form hexagons. It is more suitable for a coarse groundwork than for a filling, because it is too poor and thin compared with most fillings.

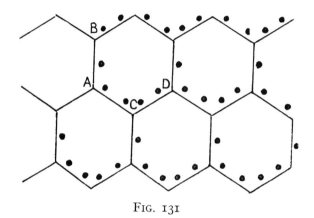

FIG. 131

It can be seen in the Victoria and Albert Museum, Lace, T22—1911.

For No. 12 S. thread make the sides of the hexagons $\frac{1}{12}$ in. long. The diagram shows where the pinholes are placed.

For the picots twist three times before making the loop and twice after the second thread has passed round the pin.

To Work the Filling. Commence with two pairs at A, make the plait and picots to B, then make a "sewing" *over* the bar above, or into pinhole of braid. It is safer to make 1 knot to keep it up in position. Plait down to next picot, then "sew" over the twisted bar just made. Plait again to A, where another sewing and knot are made. Then make plait and picots to C and on to D, where another upright bar is made, continue to end of row. Commence at X, make a similar row, sewing the upright bars to the row above.

131

Filling of Whole Stitch Blocks (*Figs.* 132 *and* 133).

This filling consists of rows of whole stitch blocks, the blocks of one row alternating with those of the rows above and beneath. The blocks (or "buds" as they would be described by Midland workers) are connected by half-stitch bars.

It can be seen in the Victoria and Albert Museum, Lace, in a lappet

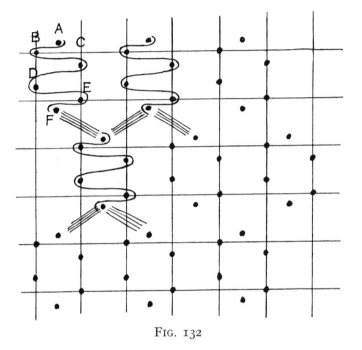

FIG. 132

T22—1911. The illustration in the small Honiton sampler, Fig. 95, space 1, was worked with No. 12 S. thread.

THE PRICKING was made so that the whole stitch blocks are one-sixteenth of an inch wide, there are six holes for each block. The four side holes are not opposite but alternate, as for a braid (see enlarged pricking). The top and bottom holes are in the middle, but a little above and below the others, this gives the finished block an oval appearance. There is $\frac{1}{16}$ in. between the blocks horizontally. The distance between the lower holes of one row and the top holes of the next is about $\frac{1}{32}$ in.

TO WORK THE FILLING. Hang four pairs at A. With the two

middle pairs make a whole stitch, twist each pair three times, and put the pin between them, enclose the pin with a whole stitch. With the two right-hand pairs make a whole stitch. With the two left-hand pairs make a whole stitch. Use the third pair from the left as leaders and, working to the left, make the whole stitch block (of course, without edge pins), twist leaders three times when passing round the pins. After enclosing the pin E, take the leaders through to the other side. Make a whole stitch with the two right-hand pairs. With the two middle pairs, make a whole stitch, twist three times, put up a pin in F, enclose pin with whole stitch. With the two right-hand pairs make a bar of four half-stitches, do the same with the two left-hand pairs. The block (in next row) under a space is made with the pairs from the two bars, one from each of the two blocks above.

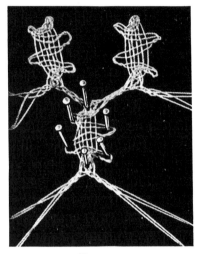

FIG. 133

A variation of this is to be seen in the same specimen in the Victoria and Albert Museum. It has a hole in the middle of each block.

A smaller arrangement is also shown in the same specimen, but this has only two holes. It is illustrated in the small Honiton sampler, Fig. 99, space 6.

The pricking for this was made so that from the middle of one block to the middle of the next, horizontally, is $\frac{1}{8}$ in. The pair of holes for the block are $\frac{1}{32}$ in. apart. The blocks of one row alternate with those of the rows above and under. It was worked with No. 12 S. thread.

Filling. Cutwork and Pinhole (Figs. 134 and 135).

This filling consists of cutworks and pinholes alternating. The leadworks are surrounded by twisted threads, coming from the pinhole above and passing to the one under it.

It can be seen in the Victoria and Albert Museum, Lace, lappet

506—1883. The illustration in the small Honiton sampler, Fig. 99, space 2, was worked with No. 12 S. thread.

THE PRICKING was made on sectional paper 16 to the inch, every other crossing being used for a pinhole.

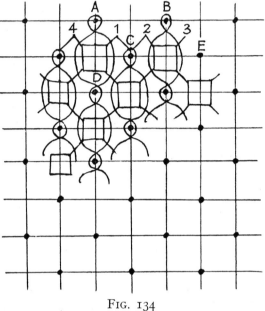

FIG. 134

TO WORK THE FILLING. Hand two pairs round a pin at *A*, twist three times, and enclose pin with a whole stitch, twist each pair twice and leave. Repeat this with two pairs hung round a pin at *B*. At a point 1, midway between *A* and *C*, hang two pairs, also hang two pairs at 2, midway between *B* and *C*, and two pairs at 3, between *B* and *E*. These last six pairs must each be twisted twice. At point 4, hang in one pair, use it with the left-hand pair from *A* to make a whole stitch, then twist the left-hand pair three times and the right-hand pair twice. With the left-hand pair from point 1 and the right-hand pair from *A* make a whole stitch; twist the right-hand pair three times and the left-hand pair twice. With the two pairs just passed through from *A* make a square lead-work, twist each pair twice, work a whole stitch with the left-hand pair and the twisted pair on the left; twist each pair twice. Work a whole stitch with the right-hand

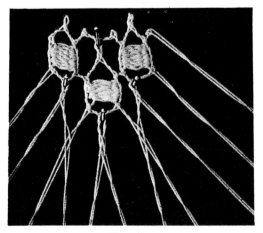

FIG. 135

pair and the twisted pair on the right; twist each pair twice. Of the last four pairs just used, cross the two middle pairs in whole stitch, put up a pin in hole *D*, twist each pair twice and enclose the pin with a whole stitch and two twists; leave. Now use the two twisted pairs hanging from 1 and 2, make a whole stitch, twist each pair twice, put up a pin in hole *C*, enclose pin with a whole stitch and two twists. These are ready for two pairs (one from either side) to pass through them for the next leadwork.

NOTE. This filling can be worked in diagonal rows from right to left, commencing at the top left-hand corner or can be worked in horizontal rows. The pairs used to make a pinhole pass round the plait and are used for the lower pinhole. The pairs used for the leadworks pass diagonally from one to the next.

Cutwork with a Hole, and a Pin Filling.

This filling is pricked and worked upon the same principal as the cushion filling. Each cutwork has a hole in the middle made by twisting the threads, therefore the horizontal rows must be much wider apart to allow of this.

It is to be seen in the Victoria and Albert Museum, Lace, 541—1875.

The illustration in the small Honiton sampler, Fig. 99, space 3, was worked with No. 12 S. thread.

THE PRICKING. Make the horizontal rows of holes $\frac{1}{8}$ in., or a little less, apart, and the vertical rows of holes $\frac{1}{16}$ in. apart.

Filling. "Four-pin Blocks" (Figs. 136 *and* 137).

This filling consists of diagonal lines of twisted threads, between which are "four-pin blocks" with a middle hole.

It can be seen in the Victoria and Albert Museum, Lace, T22,—1911.

The illustration in the small Honiton sampler, Fig. 99, space 4, was worked with No. 12 S. thread.

THE PRICKING was made upon sectional paper 16 to the inch, used diagonally, every other crossing is used for the pinhole where the twisted threads cross. Between these, four holes are pricked which would form a square of about $\frac{1}{16}$ in.

TO WORK THE FILLING. Hang two pairs at pinhole *A*, making

a half-stitch, twist three times, and enclose the pin with a half-stitch and three more twists. Hang six pairs from between *B* and *C*, cross them all in whole stitch (third pair through three pairs to the right, second pair through three pairs to the right, first pair through three pairs to the right). Divide these pairs into two parts, with the left-hand three pairs make a little six-thread plait (third pair in whole

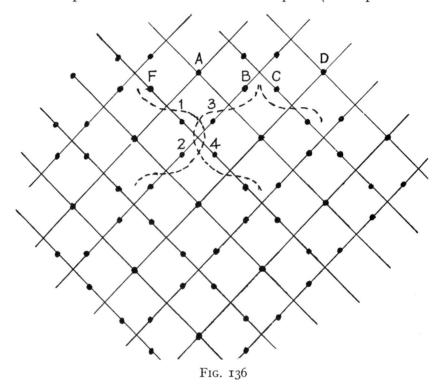

FIG. 136

stitch through two pairs, and then the third pair again through two pairs), continue plait until it is long enough to reach half-way to the top of the underneath block. Pass the right-hand twisted pair through the six plaited threads in whole stitch, twist four times, and leave.

Make another six-thread plait as above with the same three pairs, and leave. Make a similar plait with the left-hand three pairs from between *B* and *C*, hang in one pair at *D* and pass it through this plait as before. Hang three pairs from the left side of *F* and make

136

the six-thread plait, passing the left-hand twisted threads from *A* through the middle of it.

The little four-pin block is made next with the six pairs which have just passed through the twisted threads. Cross the pairs in whole stitch, pull up very closely, then divide into two equal parts. Use the left-hand threads, take the third as leader pair, pass to the

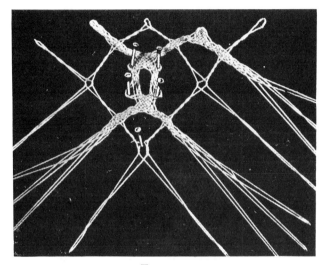

FIG. 137

left through two pairs, twist leaders three times, put up a pin in hole 1, bringing the leaders round it; work back through two pairs, the second making a turning stitch (to form the middle hole), again work out through the two pairs, twisting, and putting up pin in hole 2, work back through two pairs, leave this, and work the right-hand three pairs in the same way, then cross all the threads again in whole stitch, divide them and make the two six-thread plaits, passing twisted threads through them as before.

NOTE. It is often necessary to pull up the threads tightly or it will look too loose.

A Variety of "Toad in the Hole."

The difference between this filling and the usual Toad-in-the-hole is the sets of three holes, instead of the little "walls" of cloth-stitch bars. It can be seen in the Victoria and Albert Museum, Lace, No. 541—1875.

The illustration in small Honiton sampler, Fig. 99 (5), was worked with No. 12 S. thread.

THE PRICKING has sets of three holes placed vertically. Each set occupies $\frac{1}{16}$ in., and is $\frac{1}{4}$ in. from the next set horizontally. The rows alternate so that a set of holes in one row comes immediately over, and under, the cutworks of the upper and lower holes.

TO WORK THE FILLING. As it is worked upon the same principle as the Toad-in-the-hole, it is only necessary to explain how to work the sets of holes.

Use four pairs, each two pairs having been worked together into a bar of four half-stitches. With the two middle pairs, work a whole stitch and a twist, and put up a pin in the top hole. With each two side pairs work a whole stitch and a twist, then enclose the top pin by making a whole stitch and a twist with the two middle pairs. Put up the next pin, and then use the two side pairs to work a whole stitch and a twist. Enclose pin as before, then work the side pairs in whole stitch and a twist; put up the last pin and enclose it.

Divide the pairs, and make the half-stitch plaits ready for the twisted pairs from the cutworks to pass through.

Whole Stitch Net with Cutworks.

This filling consists of a net of twisted threads and whole stitches with cutworks placed so as to form lines or spottings.

Different varieties can be seen in the Victoria and Albert Museum, Lace, No. 506—1883.

One variety with lines of cutworks is to be seen in the small Honiton sampler (Fig. 99) in space 10, and a spotted variety in space 7 of the same sampler. Both were worked with 12 S. thread. These fillings are worked diagonally in rows from right down to left, commencing at the top left-hand corner. No pricking is needed.

TO WORK THE FILLING. Hang passive pairs at equal distances, twist each pair three times, then cross them diagonally from right to left, with a leader pair which twists three times between each passive pair and the next, and passes through them with whole stitch.

138

At the end of the row sew leaders to edge. This pair can often be left hanging as passives. For the cutworks either in rows or at intervals, work as explained in the "No Pin" filling, using the same leader thread for each cutwork to prevent them from drawing up.

Cutwork with a Hole in a Twisted Net.

This filling is a variety of "Swing" filling; it is worked diagonally and needs no pricking.

Make a row of cutworks, alternating with pairs, each of which is twisted three times. The next row is a twisted pair passing through the others in whole stitch, and twisting three times between each pair. Then make another row like the first. Every cutwork has a hole in the middle of it after the style used in "Old Honiton" and the Victoria and Albert Museum, Lace, No. 531—1875.

The filling in the small Honiton sampler, Fig. 99, space 8, was worked with No. 12 S. thread.

Filling. Cutwork and Lattice (Fig. 138).

This filling consists of rows of cutworks. In between the rows are rows of lattice work, made of twisted threads. The cutworks of one row alternate with those in the rows above and under. The illustration in the small Honiton sampler, Fig. 99, space 9, was worked with No. 12 S. thread. The cutworks are about $\frac{1}{24}$ in. square. No pricking is required.

To WORK THE FILLING. Hang up two pairs at each hole at top of filling, and enclose the pins with whole stitch. No pins are used for the filling. Of the first four pairs, twist the first and fourth three times each and leave. With the two inner pairs, make a square cutwork at the foot of the cutwork; use the threads to make whole stitches with the twisted pairs just left on the outer sides. Twist these four pairs three times each, and leave. Make two more similar cutworks with the other pairs from the top; all pairs should be twisted three times and left. Next make the lattice. To do this, work the second and third pairs together in whole stitch. Twist each pair three times and leave. Work the fourth and fifth pairs together in whole stitch. Twist three times and leave, continue thus to the end of the row. For the next row, unite every two pairs in whole stitch by working the third and fourth pairs together, then the next two, and so on to the end of the row.

Now make a row of cutworks using the pairs so that they alternate

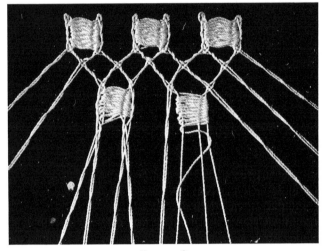

FIG. 138

with the other rows of cutworks. Before commencing the cutworks, pull up the pairs carefully into position.

The fourth and fifth pairs should be twisted once and used to weave the cutwork, and the third and sixth pairs are to be twisted three times each and used to make the whole stitches with the pairs from the foot of the cutwork. Continue to end of row. The odd pairs at either end, of course, are sewn into the braid surrounding the filling.

CHAPTER X
BUCKS "POINT GROUND"

THIS is one of the finest of the English "Trolly" laces, in which the design and grounding net are worked in conjunction with each other. The designing is somewhat limited on account of the net ground being made in slanting lines, and the clothwork straight across. For the same reason, it is more intricate to work than other laces, and requires a greater number of bobbins. The designing certainly could be carried further, and many of the old "fillings" could be used to give interest impossible to obtain otherwise than by handwork. There is much in favour of this lace. It is strong and both sides are as nearly alike as possible, which is a great advantage for many purposes. It is suitable for all kinds of ecclesiastical, household, and dress wear, requiring a fine lace. Both cotton and linen threads are used to make it with, but linen is better.

Space   POINT GROUND SAMPLER STITCHES   *Page*

1. Whole stitch or cloth work 148
2. Fancy hole 148
3. Honeycomb bud 153
4. Honeycomb bud with leadwork 156
5. Purl pin edge 149
6. Point Ground net 150
7. Point Ground net spotted with leadworks (Point d'Esprit) . 152
8. Kat stitch or French wire ground 157
9. Kat stitch spotted with leadworks 163
10. Mayflower filling (Honeycomb with cloth stitch buds) . . 164
11. Twisted half stitch. 45
12. Honeycomb 153
13. Honeycomb spotted with leadworks (inside the honeycomb holes) . 160
14. Honeycomb spotted with leadworks (instead of honeycomb holes) . 162
15. Whole stitch honeycomb spotted with leadworks (inside pinholes) . 155
16. Horizontal filling, whole stitch bars and leadworks . . . 165
17. Horizontal filling, whole stitch bars united by pin chain . . 165
18. Horizontal filling, half-stitch bars and leadworks . . . 165

FIG. 139

Before commencing Point Ground lace, it is advisable to have read through the General Notes, and to have worked through most of the Torchon part, so as to be familiar with the trolly method of pillow lace-making, in which the threads of the design are worked in and out, to and from, the grounding and fillings. I have given directions and the prickings for working two or three narrow laces,

142

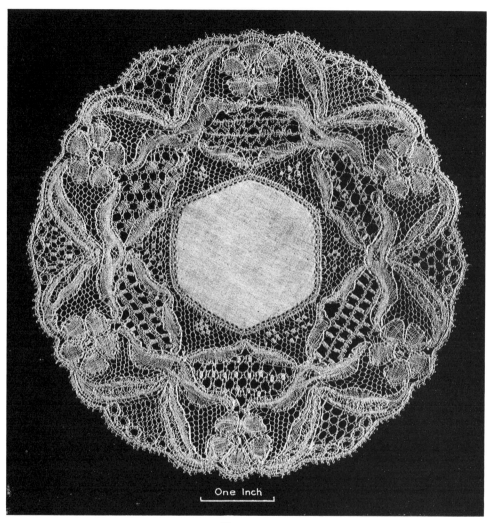

One Inch

FIG. 140

which will show how the threads travel across the lace. After this, it should be easy to copy from other patterns and to re-arrange and design fresh ones.

Bucks Point Ground Designing and Pattern Making.

If the student is likely to do much designing, or pattern making, for this lace, it will save considerable time to draw with ink upon

143

a strong drawing-paper (in order that they may be used again and again) strips of the most useful angles. Place a piece of tracing-paper upon the strip of the angle you decide to use and fasten with paper

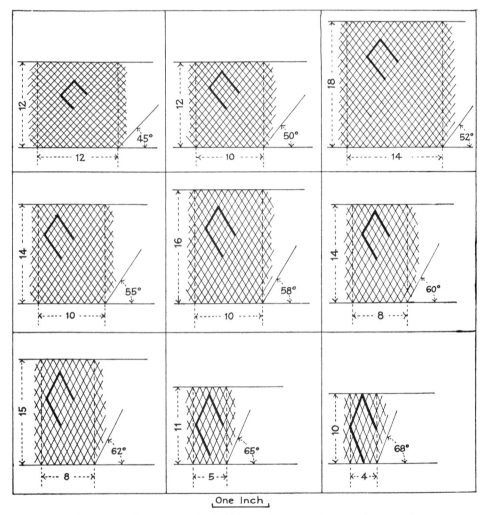

FIG. 141. TABLE OF ANGLES FOR BUCKS "POINT GROUND"

clips. Then draw your design upon the tracing-paper. This enables the designer to see exactly what shapes are possible to be worked. A great deal depends upon the angle used. If possible, refer to collections of this lace and notice the different appearances obtained

144

by the same stitch worked at various angles. After the design is drawn out upon the tracing-paper, go over it carefully, mark all the grounding pinholes with a pencil, and see that the outlining thread keeps the shape required, because, in many instances, the weight of the bobbin pulls it from the intended line. It would be better sometimes to exaggerate a point, and so prevent it from becoming too rounded in the working. Curves must, of course, be adapted in a similar way. Now pencil in the pinholes for the fillings, arranging them as symmetrically as possible. Next, dot in the pinholes for the heavier parts. These must be arranged so as to give an even appearance to the fabric, and they must also be placed so that the grounding and fillings are not pulled out of shape in working. Finally, mark in the pinholes, for any holes, or other fancy stitches, and the purl pins along the edge.

The tracing-paper can now be removed, and pinned firmly with the parchment, or pricking card, on to the pricking board, and the pricking made. The pricked pattern must have all necessary markings put in before "setting up" the work. For method of pricking repeating patterns, see Torchon lace, page 36.

Table of Angles for Bucks Point Ground.

I have drawn out a table of several angles, and described how to do it. A worker, making Bucks prickings, must first draw out a sufficient length of angled paper on which to arrange one repeat of her design. It is advisable when making first attempts to fasten a piece of tracing-paper over your angled paper for experimental purposes; otherwise, a small slip may necessitate redrawing the angles, which, at the best, is a tedious business.

To DRAW THE ANGLES. Along a line A—B (see Fig. 142) with a pair of dividers step off several equal parts (14 to the inch is the most usual for "point ground," but it must vary with the size of the thread). From one of these points (C) draw a vertical line, place the protractor upon the line A—B, and with the centre exactly at point C. Now mark off two points (X and X in illustration) at the angle required, for instance, 50 degrees on the right and 50 degrees on the left. Draw lines from point C through the points X and X, and then draw lines parallel to them from each of the other divisions on the line *A—B*. These lines cross each other at points where the pinholes are to be made.

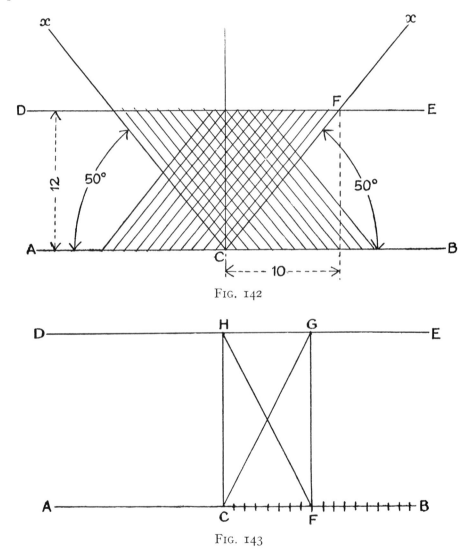

FIG. 142

FIG. 143

Another, and perhaps more accurate, way is to make your table of angles upon squared paper. Then make notes of the number of squares there are between the line *A—B*, and one upon which the crossings coincide with one of the lines of the paper (*D—E*) also note the number of squares horizontally there are between point *C* and the point where the angle from *C* meets the line of horizontal crossings *D—E* (*F* in Fig. 142).

By referring to the illustration it will be seen that there are twelve divisions (of the squared paper) vertically between the line *A—B* and the line *D—E*, and ten divisions horizontally between the vertical line from *C* and the point *F*, where the angle meets the top line *D—E*. The squares of the paper are not shown, but the numbers are given in dotted lines.

I have given this numbering on my table of angles as this method saves the trouble of using a protractor for every draft. The angle marked 62 degrees (Fig. 141) is lettered in Fig. 143 to illustrate how to use it. Draw upon plain smooth drawing-paper (the sectional kind is very confusing to make these prickings on) a horizontal line *A—B*, and mark a point *C* from which step off with dividers a number of equal parts same size spacing as the footside pins. Now make another line *D—E*, parallel to *A—B*, leaving a distance of 15 (or its multiple) of your equal spaces (see Fig. 141) between them. Connect them by a vertical line from *G* to *H*, then make another vertical line from *F* to *G*, eight spaces or same multiples as before away from the first. A line drawn from *G* to *C*, and another from *H* to *F* give the angles. The lines parallel to these can be more accurately drawn if the top line is spaced off in the same way as the lower one, instead of trusting only to parallel ruler or set squares. It will only be necessary to draw out sufficient length for one head or repeat, the method of repeating prickings is given on page 36.

The use of this table of angles will be seen by placing a piece of "point ground" net over each angle until the lines of the net and drawing coincide.

The angles drawn thicker, show the shapes that will be formed with that angle.

The page of angles on transparent paper has another use: The lace, print, or photograph of it can be placed *under* it to determine its angle which would be impossible with opaque paper.

There is a method of drafting Point Ground patterns upon squared paper, but, as so many of the pinholes have to be placed between the lines of the paper, in order to obtain the right angle, it is confusing and not always correct.

Sizes of Point Ground Threads.

For Point Ground lace both linen and cotton thread[1] are used, but the linen is much the better.

I am giving a few sizes in linen threads and gimp to use with them. This will be a little guide, but much depends upon the pattern, the weight of the bobbins, and the way in which the bobbins are handled. The first is the most suitable for a beginner.

For 12 to the inch pricking use 200 linen thread and No. 24 gimp.
,, 14 ,, ,, ,, ,, 250 ,, ,, ,, ,, 30 ,,
,, 16 ,, ,, ,, ,, 300 ,, ,, ,, ,, 36 ,,

Point Ground Clothing or Heavier Parts.

The heavier parts of Point Ground are worked either in whole stitch or half-stitch. The working of these is described in the General Notes on pages 19 and 21.

The clothing of Point Ground is of a much lighter texture than that of the Devon lace. Should it become too thin, other bobbins may be added in parts and taken out later, but it is not practical to be continually hanging in and cutting out extra pairs.

When hanging in fresh threads, the bobbins must be wound in pairs, and hung in round the gimp. When twisted and worked in with others they are imperceptible. There seems to be no special method for this, but take care that the weight of the new bobbins does not pull the lace out of shape.

To take out bobbins: Just throw them out over the back of the pillow so that they do not drag the lace, later they can be cut off, being tied first if necessary for strength.

---

[1] It is not possible to give comparative sizes in slip thread, as I find the quality and size vary considerably, according to where it is purchased, although it is all quoted as "the best." The poorer quality is not regular, mostly coarser in size, rough and fluffy, and breaks quickly. It is a pity there is not some satisfactory method of labelling, as counting the number of slips, or skips, in a skein is not reliable.

148

Fancy Holes and Spotted Grounds.

There are very few fancy holes in Point Ground lace.

Their chief use is to break up a large plain surface of clothing. They consist of a few pinholes, four or six, placed so that one is at

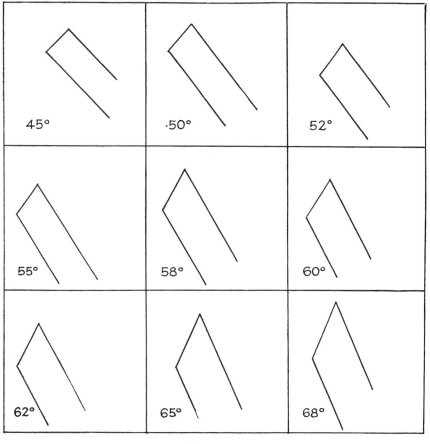

FIG. 144

the top and another at the bottom, and either one or two holes on both sides. For the top hole the leader and the nearest passive pair, twist and work together enclosing a pin. Then these pairs form leaders which travel out and back, and then make what the Devon workers call "winkie pins," they are just twisted as they pass round the pin. Then these leaders are once more worked out and

149

back again. At the bottom they unite round a pin in the same way as at the top, and one leader pair hangs so as to form passive threads while the other leader pair continues to weave across and across.

Centres of flowers often consist of a plait or leadwork. Sometimes a simple crossing of threads is all that is necessary.

Very effective centres can be arranged by the judicious use of part of a filling, but a few trials, sketched on to the design will soon show which is best for a particular space. Open veins to leaves are pretty when filled with a ladder of crossed threads like mittens (see Honiton, part page 94), or a succession of plaits. Wider spaces can be varied by a row of honeycomb pinholes, on both sides of the plaits.

A reference to good specimens of lace will give many ideas which can be adapted to the workers requirements.

A special feature of this lace is the spottings or powderings on or in the ground net. They may be just a point d'esprit plait or plaits forming patterns at intervals, or a little bud, leaf, or blossom of whole stitch and outlined with gimp.

Always keep the spottings distinct from the design. The simpler ones are often the best.

Purl Edge.

The picots used in Point Ground lace are described on page 26 of the General Notes, they are often called "Turn Pins" by the Midland workers. The double picot is necessary, owing to the fine thread used. The picots used for the outer edge differ a little from those occasionally found in the fillings.

To Work the Edge Picot. Bring the leaders out to the edge. Twist them twice, and work a whole stitch with the edge pair. Twist the outside pair five times and make the double picot, then make a whole stitch with the next pair. Twist these pairs twice each and continue the weaving.

Picots for fillings are made without the double twists before and after which form a hole, the whole, or half-stitch, before and after being all that is necessary to secure it.

Gimp Threads.

"Gimp" is the heavy "shiny" flax thread used for outlining, larger bobbins being mostly used to carry it.

Gimps are not worked in pairs like the other threads, but woven in and out those threads which connect the heavy work with the grounding.

Bucks Point Ground or Trolly Net (Figs. 145 and 146).

This net is used as a grounding to nearly all Bucks Point lace. Sometimes it is used as a filling, and for either purpose it can be varied by the use of plaits.

When it is spotted it is called "Point d'Esprit net." It will be found in most lace collections. Both plain and spotted nets are to be seen in the Bucks sampler, Fig. 139, in spaces 6 and 7.

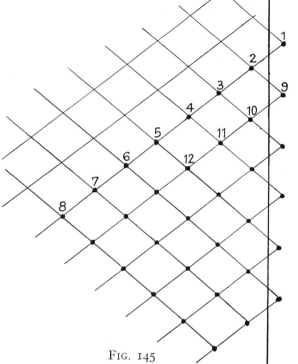

FIG. 145

They are worked with (250) linen thread. Pricked 12 to the inch, and angled at 52 degrees.

THE PRICKING is made in diagonal rows.

THE STITCH consists of a half-stitch and two extra twists. A pin is put up between the pairs but not enclosed.

TO WORK THE NET with edge braid called the "foot side."

One pair of bobbins should hang from just above 1. Two pairs from between 1 and 2; these are the edge passives. Two pairs from between 2 and 3, and one pair from between each pinhole and the next of the top line. Use the fourth pair from the right side as leaders and work whole stitch through the edge passives. Twist the leaders three times. Put up a pin in hole 1, so that the leaders pass behind it. Make a whole stitch with the leader pair and the end pair, twist each pair three times.[1] Work the second pair from the right through the two passive pairs in whole stitch. Twist the leaders three times and put up a pin in hole 2 so that the leaders pass behind it. Use the leaders with the next pair on the left, make a net stitch (half-stitch and two extra twists), but do not put up a pin. Drop the

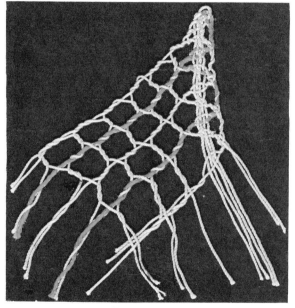

FIG. 146

right-hand pair, and use the next pair on the left to make another net stitch. Put up a pin in hole 3. Continue these net stitches and pin to the end of the row, each time dropping the right-hand pair and using the next pair on the left.

Now remove the pins used to hang the threads from, and pull all the bobbins down carefully into position. Each row is worked

[1] Many workers twist the edge pair only twice. The number of twists should depend upon the size of the thread used. When only two twists are used, the pairs coming to and from the net must only be twisted twice. As the net stitch leaves a treble twist, it is better to use the three twists at the edge whenever the thread is fine enough to allow it without kinking.

the same way, commencing with the fourth pair from the right as leaders in order to weave through the edge braid. It is very necessary that each pair of threads for this net is twisted three times. A red thread is used in the diagram to show the course of the leader threads.■

Bucks Point Ground or Trolly Net. Second Diagram (Figs. 147 *and* 148).

It is sometimes advisable to commence from a line straight across the pattern instead of at the net angle.

The second diagram illustrates this method and also shows how to work the plaits for spotting the net.

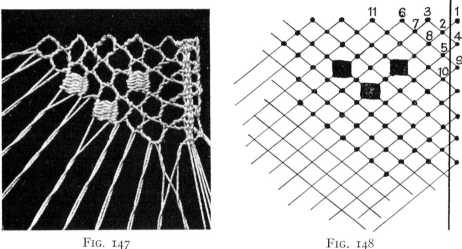

FIG. 147   FIG. 148

Hang one pair just above 1.

Hang three pairs from between 1 and 2, the two right-hand pairs to use as braid passives.

Hang two pairs from 3. Twist these two pairs each three times.

Use the pair on the right of these as leaders to work in whole stitch through the 2 braid passive pairs.

Twist the leaders three times. Put up a pin in hole 1 so that the leaders pass behind it. With the leader pair and the end pair, make a whole stitch. Twist each pair three times. Work the second pair from the right in whole stitch, through the two passive pairs. Twist the leaders three times. Put up a pin in hole 2 so that the

* Here shaded grey.

leaders pass behind it. Then make a net stitch (half-stitch and two extra twists) with it and the next pair from 3, and leave. The pin supporting the braid passives, must now be removed, and the threads pulled down into position.

Hang two pairs round a pin at 6. Twist each pair three times. Use the right-hand pair with the next pair from 3. Make a net stitch, and put up a pin between the pairs at 7. With the right-hand pair from 7, and the left-hand pair from 2, make a net stitch. Put up a pin at 8. Use the fourth pair from the right as leaders, and work through the edge passives, twist, put up a pin in 4, and make the edge stitch.

Work back again, twist, put up a pin in hole 5 so that the leaders pass behind it, make a net with it and the next pair on the left, and leave.

Now hang two more pairs on a pin at 11 and proceed as before, working in slanting lines, down to the edge braid.

It does not matter in which direction this net is worked providing it is worked in slanting rows.

Plaits in Net Ground.

The plait takes the place of a pinhole, so that when making the pricking omit the pinhole where the plait is to be, and make a little spot of ink in its place.

When the net is worked down to the spot indicated, use the two pairs to weave the plait, instead of making the net stitch; twist each pair three times, leaving the one pair ready for the next row of net, and continue to work the usual net stitches with the other pair.

Bucks "Honeycomb" Net or Filling (Figs. 149 and 150).

This stitch is to be found in nearly all Bucks lace.

It is used either as a filling or ground net, also it can be just the simple stitch or varied by the use of plaits. The illustration in the Bucks sampler, Fig. 139, space 12, was worked with No. 250 linen thread, the pricking being made 12 to the inch and angled at 52 degrees.

THE PRICKING is made in rows at the same angle as the design, but every other row has its alternate holes missed.

THE STITCH consists of a half-stitch and one extra twist, the pin put up between the pairs and enclosed with half-stitch and one extra twist.

To Work the Filling. With two pairs from *A* and *B* passed

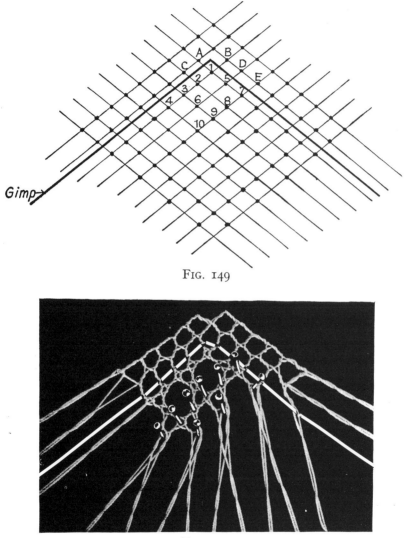

FIG. 149

FIG. 150

from the net (with the gimp passed between and twisted twice), make a half-stitch and one more twist; put up pin in hole 1 and enclose with half-stitch and one more twist, drop the right-hand pair and use

155

another pair from the net at *C*. Work another honeycomb stitch enclosing pin (at hole 2) as before. Again drop the right-hand pair, and take the next left-hand pair from the net continuing until the row is finished.

For the second or short row use a pair from hole 1 and a pair from the net, and with the gimp passed between, from the net at *D*, make the honeycomb stitch, put up pin in hole 5, enclose it with honeycomb stitch, and leave both pairs.

Take two fresh pairs from holes 2 and 3, to make the next stitch, enclosing pinhole 6. These are left, and again two fresh pairs used for the next hole. Continue to the end of row, and then make another long row. The pair from hole 5 and a pair from the net making hole 7 then continue by dropping the right-hand pair and using the next pair on the left.

Bucks Filling. "Whole Stitch Honeycomb" (Figs. 151–153).

This filling is more often found in old than modern lace, and can be seen in the Victoria and Albert Museum, Lace, No. T234—1916. It is pricked and worked in exactly the same way as "Honeycomb," and can be varied by the use of plaits; the only difference being in the stitch.

The illustration in the Bucks sampler, Fig. 139, space 15, has plaits in some of the holes, and was worked with No. 250 linen thread, the pricking made 12 to the inch and angled at 52 degrees.

THE PRICKING is made in rows at the same angle as the design, every other hole in the alternate rows being missed.

THE STITCH consists of a whole stitch and one twist, a pin put up between the pairs and enclosed with a whole stitch and one twist.

TO WORK THE FILLING. First or long row: With two pairs from *A* and *B* passed from the net with the gimp passed between and twisted once, make a whole stitch and one twist, put up pin in hole 1 and enclose with a whole stitch and one twist, drop the right-hand pair and use another pair from the net at *C*, work another stitch pin in hole 2 and enclosing as before, again drop right-hand pair, and take the next left-hand pair from the net, continuing until the row is finished. For the second: Use a pair from hole 1 and a pair

156

from the net with the gimp passed between from the net at *D*. Make the stitch, put up pin in hole 5, and enclose it; leave both pairs.

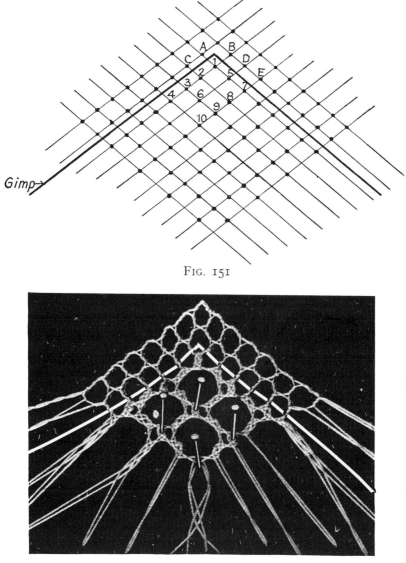

FIG. 151

FIG. 152

Take two fresh pairs from holes 2 and 3 for the next pinhole 6. These are left, and again two fresh ones used for the next hole.

Continue to end of row and then make another long row, the pair from hole 5 and one from the net making hole 7. Then continue by dropping the right-hand pair and using the next pair to the left.

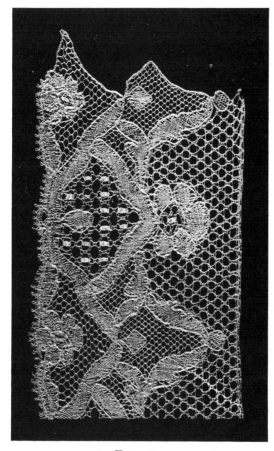

FIG. 153

Bucks Kat Stitch or Wire Ground (Figs. 154–155).

This stitch is used as a ground net or filling, and it is sometimes varied by the use of plaits. It can be seen in most lace collections. The illustration in the Bucks sampler, Fig. 139, space 8, and grounding of edging, page 157, was worked with No. 250 linen thread, the pricking was made 6 to the inch and angled at 52 degrees. It can be made without a pricking, but requires more practice.

THE PRICKING is made and the stitches are worked diagonally. Four pairs of bobbins are required for one pinhole, two of which are used with two fresh ones for the next pinhole.

THE STITCH requires four pairs, each pair twisted once; consists of a half-stitch with the two middle pairs, a pin put up between them, and enclosed with a half-stitch, then make a whole stitch and one twist with the two right-hand pairs, and a whole stitch and one twist with the two left-hand pairs.

TO WORK THE FILLING. With four pairs from the net at *A*, *B*, *C*, and *D*, with the gimp passed through and each pair twisted once,

158

make a half-stitch with the two middle pairs, put up a pin between them at 1, and enclose it with a half-stitch. Now make a whole stitch and 1 twist with the two right-hand pairs, and a whole stitch

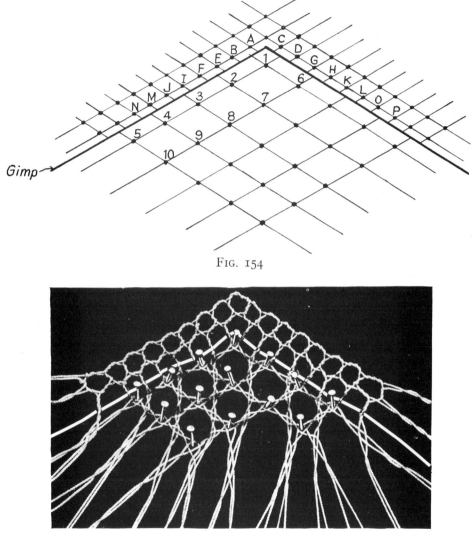

FIG. 154

FIG. 155

and one twist with the two left-hand pairs, leave the two right-hand pairs. Take the two left-hand pairs and 2 fresh ones on the left in the gimp passed between them, from the net at E and F, each twisted

159

once. Make the stitch with these, putting up pin in hole 2, also working the whole stitch and twist with the outside pairs as before. Again, drop the two right-hand pairs and take two more from the net, continuing until the row is finished.

The second row is the same, for the pinhole 6 use two pairs from net on right side and two pairs from hole 1 of first row.

Point Ground Fillings.

The fancy stitches called fillings, are sometimes used in the various spaces surrounded by parts of the design, and sometimes within the design so as to form the centres to flowers and leaves.

They lighten the lace and give variety, but must be very carefully chosen. Unlike Honiton, the fillings are worked in as the lace proceeds. The threads of the surrounding parts come out from one side, travel through the filling, and are taken in on the other side.

The same number of threads are used as in the grounding. Occasionally, a finer net is used as a filling, but it is so arranged that the enclosing heavier work carries the larger number of threads also, and, if possible, the design should be arranged so that these extra threads can be worked through the whole length of lace.

Pins must be used for all fillings, most of which are pricked at the angle of the ground net. A few fillings are worked vertically and appear horizontal when the lace is used, and also a few are worked at the angle of 45 degrees. In describing the fillings, I have given instructions for working one repeat. A red thread is used to illustrate the gimp outlining of the surrounding part, and it is passed through the threads in the same way as a gimp would be.[*] Point ground fillings cannot be arranged to curve or radiate, but must keep strictly to geometrical lines and angles.

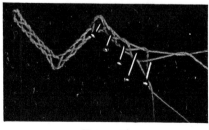

FIG. 156

Pin Chain (Fig. 156).

This is a succession of honeycomb stitches, with a pin between each one and the next. It forms lines in any direction, and is

* Here solid white.

arranged in various ways in conjunction with other stitches for fillings. It is used to connect the bars in sampler, space 17. Four threads are necessary. Make the usual honeycomb stitch of a half-stitch and one extra twist, put up a pin in the top hole between the pairs. Enclose pin with another honeycomb stitch. Put up another pin, and so on.

PRICKING. The holes should be a little closer together than the usual point ground; about five holes to four of point ground is a good size.

Bucks Filling. Honeycomb with Plaits (Fig. 157).

The honeycomb net or filling is explained on page 153, and the method of weaving a plait is given on page 22 of the General Notes.

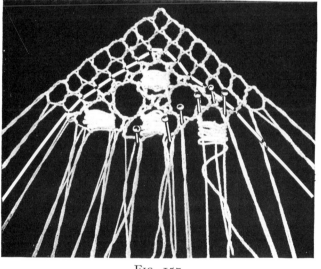

FIG. 157

One of the chief fillings of Point Ground lace is the honeycomb net spotted with plaits. The spotting can be arranged in several ways.

The first arrangement described here has the plaits worked into the honeycomb holes, therefore the usual honeycomb pricking is used with the addition of little square spots of ink to denote a plait. In the one described the plaits are spaced alternately, but other arrangements are easily worked out.

It is shown in the Northampton Museum with a plait in the honeycomb holes.

It is illustrated in space 13 in the Point Ground sampler, and in the Kat Stitch edging, page 157.

To Work the Filling. With two pairs from *A* and *B* of the net with the gimp thread passed between, make a honeycomb stitch. Put up a pin in 1. Enclose it with a honeycomb stitch. Drop the right-hand pair, and bring another pair from the net, passing the gimp through as before. Use this new pair with the left-hand pair from 1, for another honeycomb stitch, putting up the pin at 2 and enclosing it with honeycomb stitch. Continue thus until the long row is finished.

Take the right-hand pair from 1 and a fresh pair from the net, passing the gimp between and make a honeycomb stitch at 5. Enclose with honeycomb stitch. Now use the left-hand pair from 5 and the right-hand pair from 2, and weave the plait. Make a honeycomb stitch with the left-hand pair from the plait and the right-hand pair from 3. Put up a pin in 6, and enclose it with a honeycomb stitch. Continue this short row to the end, making plaits where desired. The third row is the usual long row of honeycomb stitches which takes in the right-hand pairs from every plait, making them secure.

Whole stitch honeycomb can be used with very good result, instead of the usual honeycomb stitches.

Bucks Filling. Honeycomb with Plaits (Another Variety.)

Second Arrangement. This variety has the plait made between any two honeycomb holes. In the one described, the plaits are placed alternately, but other arrangements are easily worked out.

It can be seen in the Victoria and Albert Museum, Lace, No. T287—1913, and another arrangement is illustrated in the Bucks sampler, Fig. 139, space 14.

The Pricking is arranged as for honeycomb, but omit the pinhole where a plait is required, putting a square spot of ink instead to denote a plait.

To Work the Filling. With two pairs from *A* and *B* of the net, with the gimp passed between, make a honeycomb stitch. Put

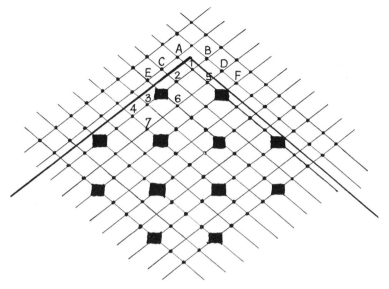

FIG. 158

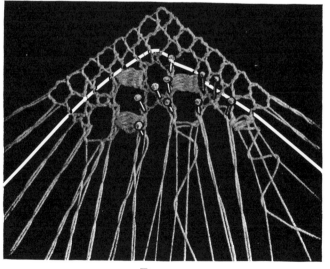

FIG. 159

up a pin in 1. Enclose it with a honeycomb stitch. Drop the right-hand pair and bring another pair from the net, passing the gimp through as before. Use this new pin with the left-hand pair from 1 for another honeycomb stitch, putting up the pin at 2, and enclosing it with a honeycomb stitch.

Bring another pair from the net at *E*, and pass the gimp through. Use this new pair with the left-hand pair from 2 to weave the plait. Put the right-hand pair aside, and use the left-hand pair with another pair from the net.

Continue honeycomb pinholes and plaits until the row is finished.

Work the short row in the usual way.

The next row is made like the first, but the plaits should be spaced so that they alternate.

Whole stitch honeycomb can take the place of the usual honeycomb with very good result.

Bucks Filling of Spotted Kat Stitch (Fig. 160).

Kat stitch is explained on page 158, and the method of weaving a plait on page 22 of the General Notes. Kat stitch is very pretty

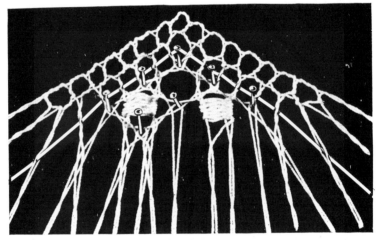

FIG. 160

as a filling if spotted with plaits. One variety can be seen in the Bucks sampler, space 9, and the same one is explained fully, but other varieties can be arranged as desired.

To Work Spotted Kat Stitch.

Proceed as for Kat Stitch, after the pin is put up and enclosed. The whole stitches with twists are worked on both sides. Use the two middle pairs to weave the plait. The stitches are not worked at the foot of the plaits until the next row is made, so great care must be taken to keep the plaits from drawing up.

Bucks Filling. Mayflower (Fig. 161).

This filling although very easy is one of the most effective.

It consists of little blocks of cloth stitch alternating with honeycomb holes. It can be seen in the Victoria and Albert Museum, Lace,

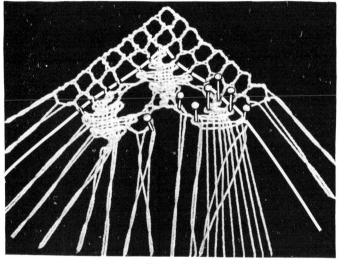

FIG. 161

No. T233—1916, and is illustrated in the Bucks sampler, Fig. 139, space 10.

THE PRICKING is the same as for honeycomb.

TO WORK THE FILLING. For the whole-stitch block at the top use the six middle pairs from the net ground. Pass the gimps between them and twist each pair once. With the two middle pairs make a whole stitch. Put up a pin in between them in hole 1. Then, using the right-hand pair as leaders, twist them twice and work back through two pairs. This takes in the other pair from C. Put up a pin in 2. Twist leaders twice and work back again to the other side and take in the pair from D, putting up a pin in 5, and twisting the leaders. Work across and across in this way, taking in pairs

165

until pinhole 7 has been worked. Then leave the pairs out again until the lowest pin, 9, has been enclosed. Each pair left out must be twisted twice. Use the pair left out from 3, and another pair from the net with the gimp passed through, and twisted twice. Make a honeycomb hole at 4 and leave. With the pair left out at 6 and the next pair on the right coming from the lowest hole of the cloth-stitch block, work a honeycomb hole at 10. This completes one repeat of the first row.

Use the pair from 4 and a new pair from the net to commence the next block and continue to the end of the row. The next row is just the usual short row of honeycomb holes bringing in a new pair from the net to commence with. This completes one repeat.

Whole stitch honeycomb can be used instead of honeycomb stitch. Another variety has two pin chain holes in place of the honeycomb hole, that is between one block and the next, but this requires two holes to be made in the pricking instead of 1.

Other varieties can be made by pricking to the angle of 45 degrees, and enlarging the blocks to four holes on every side instead of three.

Horizontal Fillings (Figs. 162 and 163).

These fillings consist of very narrow braid, connected by plaits or pin-chain. They are especially suitable for corner spaces, as their appearance adds strength to the design.

The braid is worked with three pairs in either whole or half-stitch. The pinholes of the braid are just twisted leaders without any edge pair, like the "winkie pins" of Devon lace.

It can be seen in the Victoria and Albert Museum, Lace, No. 1142—75, and is illustrated in spaces 16, 17, and 18 of the Bucks sampler, Fig. 139. The pricking is arranged upon the same angle as the net grounding so that the number of threads from the ground will carry through and out again in order to continue the ground without alteration. The enlarged pricking will show which holes are necessary to be pricked. Between every two sets of the braid holes and the next two, mark the position of the plaits with ink.

To Work the Filling. Pass the gimps through the six middle pairs from the net ground and twist the two middle pairs twice.

166

Make a honeycomb hole at pin 1. (This is worked to keep the gimp in position and has nothing to do with the filling.) Use the left-hand end pair of the middle six pairs as leaders, and work through two pairs. Twist leaders twice and put up a pin in 2. Work back again through two pairs to 3. Then work to 4 and leave. Use the right-hand end pair of the middle six pairs as leaders, and work another whole stitch braid until the pin is put up at 7. With the two leader pairs from 4 and 7, weave the plait which should be as wide as possible and not square. Continue to work the little braids, using the same leaders as before. The next plaits will be made from the outer edges of these braids, and will unite with the next two braids which, of course, must be worked with three fresh pairs from the ground on both sides.

These fillings vary according to the spacing of the plaits.

Those with half-stitch braids are very light and pretty.

Occasionally, horizontal braids are connected by means of three pin-chain stitches travelling across and across in a zigzag manner. For this, the braids will need to be pricked two holes farther apart, to allow of the extra pairs of threads from the ground necessary to make the pin-chain.

Fillings for Small Spaces.

PIN STITCH. Both the ordinary Torchon ground, and the twisted half-stitch ground are used to fill spaces where honeycomb is too large. The prickings are made at the same angle as the point net ground, which gives rather a different appearance to the stitches.

They are shown in spaces 11 and 17 of the Bucks sampler, Fig. 139.

COAT OF MAIL. This is also suitable for small spaces.

It is pricked in squares of the same size as the point net ground. A whole stitch is made, and each pair twisted once. The pin put up and enclosed with whole stitch. Two or three twists (according to the size of thread) are made between each pin and the next. The rows are worked alternately right to left, then left to right.

I have described the chief fillings. After working these, the student should have no difficulty in copying others which are to be found in old Point Ground laces.

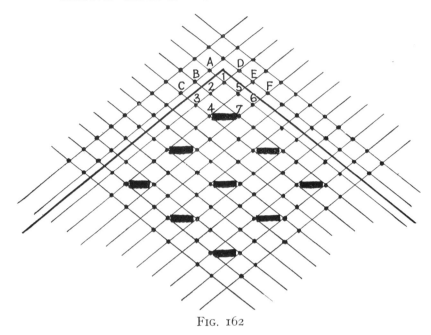

FIG. 162

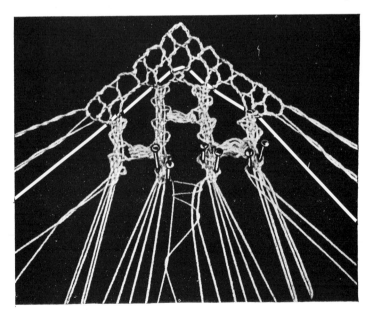

FIG. 163

Point Ground Insertion No. 1 (Figs. 164–166).

Twenty-two pairs of bobbins and two gimps are required.

Hang two pairs round a pin at 1. Twist them twice, make a whole stitch, twist twice, and leave. Hang two pairs as edge passives from a temporary pin at point X, and leave. Hang two pairs round each pin at 2 and 3, twist them three times, and leave. Use the second pair from the left side as leaders; work them in whole stitch through the edge passives, twist them three times and put up a pin in 4 so that the twisted leaders pass behind it.

Now make a net stitch (half-stitch and two extra twists) with these leaders and the next pair on the right. Do not put up a pin,

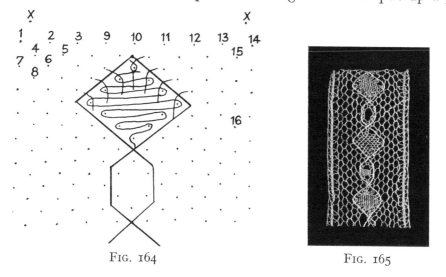

FIG. 164   FIG. 165

but leave them and take the right-hand pair from 2 and the left-hand pair from 3, make another net stitch, putting up a pin in 5, use the left of these pairs and the next pair on the left. Make a net stitch, put up a pin in 6, and leave both pairs.

Take the fourth pair from the left as leaders, work out through the passives and twist the leaders three times. Put up a pin in 7, so that the twisted leaders pass behind it. Make a whole stitch with the leaders and the edge pair, twist both pairs three times and work the second or inside pair again through the passives; twist leaders three times and put up a pin in 8 so that the leaders pass behind it

169

as before, and make the net stitch with the twisted leaders and the next pair on their right, then leave.

Begin at the top and hang two pairs from a pin at 9. Proceed as before to twist and make the net stitches diagonally down

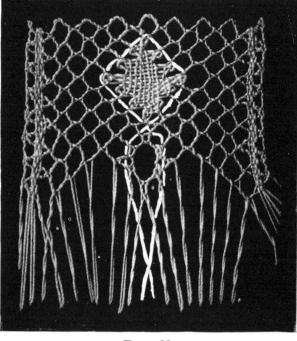

FIG. 166

to the edge. Work the edge and leave. Then hang two pairs at 10, and work another row to the edge, also work the edge and leave.

Hang two pairs round each of the three pins at 11, 12, and 13, working the diagonal rows of net down to the gimp line.

Next, hang the two edge passives (for the footing on the right side of insertion) from a temporary pin at *X*.

Hang two pairs round a pin at 14 (one as edge pair, the other as leaders). Twist these pairs and make a whole stitch about the pin and twist them again, taking the inner pair as leaders through the passives, twist and put up the pin in 15, making the net stitch

170

afterwards with the next pair as described before. Continue to work net and edging until a pin has been put up at 16.

To work the whole stitch lozenge: Hang the gimp pair on a temporary pin in the middle of the work. Pass each gimp outwards through four pairs, and twist each pair once.

With the two middle pairs make a whole stitch, put up a pin in the top hole between them, remove temporary pin for the gimp. Use the right-hand pair as leaders, twist them twice and work whole stitch through two pairs on the left. This takes in a new pair from the grounding. Twist the leaders twice, put up the pin, and work across to other side. Continue to work across and across, taking in a pair from the ground at every pin until the widest part is reached. Leave out the pairs again until the lowest pin is enclosed. Twist each pair once and pass the gimp threads through until they meet. Cross them and leave. Twist each pair three times, and continue the net ground, using the eight pairs coming from the gimp each in turn as leaders for the net work, working diagonally down to both edges.

For the honeycomb bud, commence where the gimps cross. Pass each gimp through two pairs on each side, twisting the pairs twice. With the two middle pairs make a honeycomb stitch (half-stitch and one extra twist). Put up a pin in top hole. Enclose with a honeycomb stitch and leave the right-hand pair. Use the left-hand pair with the next pair on the left, make another honeycomb stitch. Put up a pin in next hole. Enclose it with honeycomb stitch, then pass the gimp through the left-hand pair of these pairs, twist and use it with the next pair on its left, in order to make a net stitch. Pass the gimp through the right-hand pair of these two pairs, twist twice and use it with the next pair on the right. Make another honeycomb stitch. Put up the pin under the last. Enclose with honeycomb stitch. Pass the gimp through one pair, twist for net, and leave. Work the opposite holes in a similar way. To close the honeycomb ring or bud: Use the two middle pairs; make a honeycomb stitch. Put up the pin in the lowest hole. Enclose with honeycomb stitch. Pass the gimp threads each through one pair and cross the gimps. Twist the pairs for net, and work the three rows of grounding on both sides. This completes one repeat.

Point Ground Edging No. 2 (*Figs.* 167–169).

This edging requires 21 pairs of bobbins and two gimp threads.

Hang two pairs round the pin at 1. Twist them three times and leave. Hang two pairs round the pin at 2. Twist these three times and leave. Now with the right-hand pair from 1 and the left-hand pair from 2, make a net stitch (half-stitch and two more twists). Put up a pin in 3 and leave.

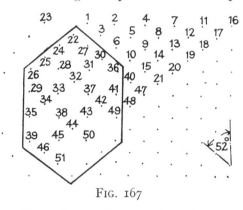

FIG. 167

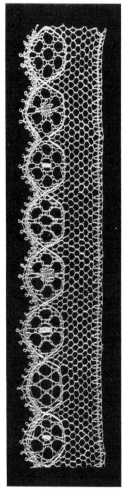

FIG. 168

Hang two pairs round a pin at 4. Twist them three times and leave. Use the right-hand pair from 2, and the left-hand pair from 4, to make a net. Put up a pin in 5 and leave. With the right-hand pair from 3, and the left-hand pair from 5, make a net stitch. Put up a pin in 6 and leave. Hang two pairs at 7. With the left of these pairs, and the next pair on their left (right-hand pair from 4), make the next net stitch. Put up the pin at 8. Make net stitches and put up pins in 9 and 10, then leave. Hang two pairs as before from 11, and work net stitches, putting up pins at 12, 13, 14, and 15. Hang two pairs from a pin at 16, so that they form a whole stitch round the pin (explained on page 14). Twist these pairs three times each, and leave. Hang two pairs from a temporary pin to use as foot side passives. Use the left-hand pair from 16 as leaders, and work through the two passive pairs in whole stitch. Twist the leaders three times, put up a pin in 17 so that the twisted leaders pass behind it. Use these leaders with the next pair on their left and make a net stitch. Do not put up the pin, but leave. Use the same leader pair and make a net stitch with the next pair on the left. Put up a pin in 18. Make three more net stitches, putting

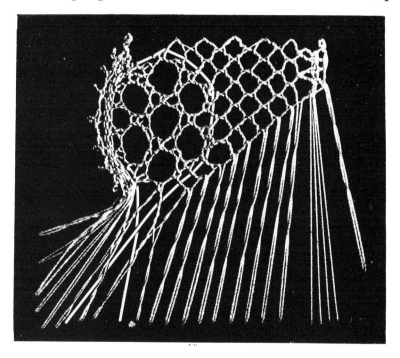

FIG. 169

pins in 19, 20, and 21, then leave. Remove the temporary pins and pull the foot passives carefully down into position.

Hang the gimps from a temporary pin above 22. Pass the right-hand gimp through the four pairs (from 1, 3, 6, and 10), and leave them twisted ready for honeycomb.

Hang five pairs also from a temporary pin, so that they hang on the outer side of the gimps. Pass the outside gimp through one pair, twist for honeycomb, and leave.

Put a pin in hole 23. Hang two pairs round it; twist them five times (in order to form a picot); work them together in whole stitch, and twist them twice. Leave the outside pair, and work the other pair through the next four pairs in whole stitch. Pass the gimp through them, twist for honeycomb, and leave.

Make a honeycomb stitch (half-stitch and one extra twist) with the pair from 1 and the next pair on the left. Put up a pin in 22 and enclose it. Leave the right-hand pair, and make another honeycomb stitch with the left-hand pair and the next pair on the left. Put up a pin in 24. Enclose it and leave.

The temporary pins must now be removed and the threads pulled carefully down into position.

With the second and third pairs from the left make a whole stitch. Twist the outer pair twice. Work it with the edge pair, and make a double picot, whole stitch, and twists, bringing the leaders through three pairs, pass the gimp through, twist and make a honeycomb stitch with the next pair on the right. Put up the pin in 25. Enclose it and leave.

Again, take the second and third pairs from the left; make a whole stitch, twist, make the purl pin edge, and bring the leaders back through two pairs, pass the gimp through, twist, and make a honeycomb stitch with the next pair on the right. Put up the pin in 26. Enclose it and bring the outside gimp through one pair. Work this pair out and make the purl pin at the edge, then work it back again.

Pass the gimp through, twist for honeycomb, and leave. With the pair from 22 and the next pair on the right (from 3) work the honeycomb hole 27, and leave both pairs.

Use the two next pairs on the left, work the honeycomb hole 28, and leave. Again, use two fresh pairs on the left and make the honeycomb hole 29. The outside pair of these two pairs is worked out to the edge, used to make the purl, and then brought back. After passing the gimp through, leave them twisted for honeycomb. Use the pair from 27 and the pair next on the right, for honeycomb hole 30, then continue to make honeycomb holes, as before, down to 35. Take the leaders out to the edge and back. After this work the short row of honeycomb holes 36, 37, 38, and 39, using the pair from 30 and the next on the right for 36. At the end of the row take the end pair out to the edge, and bring it back so as to leave it as the third pair from the end. The right-hand pair from 36 must pass the gimp. Twist and make a net stitch with the next pair on the right, putting a pin in 40. Pass the gimp through the left of these pairs, and use it with the next pair on the right for honeycomb hole 41. Continue honeycomb holes down to 46. Now pass the gimp through the end pair, and work them out to the edge, make the purl pin and return so as to leave them as third pair from the left. The right-hand gimp is passed through the pair from 41, which is twisted and left for a net stitch.

Now work the net holes 47 and 48, bringing the gimp through the end pair. Work the honeycomb holes 49, 50, and 51. Work the end pair out to the edge, make the purl, and bring it back again, leaving it as third pair.

Begin at the foot side, working the fourth pair from the end through the passives. Make the edge stitch. Work back through the passives, and twist three times. Put up a pin behind the twisted leaders, and afterwards make a net stitch with the next pair, without putting up another pin. Continue this row of net. For the last hole the gimp is passed through a pair from the honeycomb; this pair is twisted and used for the net, and the gimp again passed through it. The row of four honeycomb holes is now worked. Pass the right-hand gimp through four pairs, which must be left twisted ready for the net ground. Pass the left-hand gimp through one pair. Twist this pair twice, also twist the next pair on the left twice. Use these to make a whole stitch, twist each pair twice and leave. Cross the gimps. Make the next row of Point Ground net. Pass each gimp through one pair, which are ready to use for the top honeycomb hole of the second head.

The third pair from the left side will be found ready to bring through for the next honeycomb hole.

Point Ground Edging No. 3 (Figs. 170 and 171).

This edging requires 20 pairs of bobbins and 2 gimp threads.

Hang a pair of gimps above 3, two pairs over the gimp on the left side and eight more pairs outside on the left.

Commence by working the edge and Point Ground net from 1 down to 2. Pass the right-hand gimp through the end pair, which is next twisted and used with the next pair on the left (coming from the other gimp). Make a honeycomb stitch at 3 and leave. Work

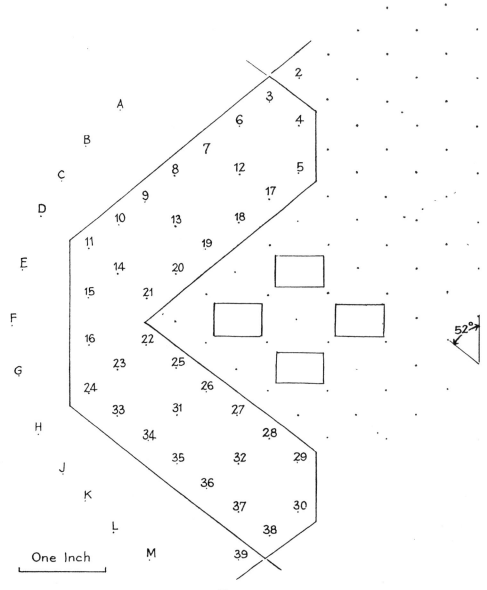

FIG. 170

One Inch

the second row of ground net. Pass the gimp through the end pair which is twisted and then used with the next pair on the left to work the honeycomb at 4. The gimp is now passed through the end pair, which are twisted for the ground net and left. Work the third row of ground net. Pass gimp through the end pair, twist, and use it with the next pair on the left for honeycomb at 5. Again, pass gimp through the right-hand pair, twist for ground net and leave. Use the pair from hole 3 and the next pair on the left (coming from the gimp) and work the honeycomb at 6.

Use the third pair from left side, weave it in whole stitch through five pairs. Pass the gimp through it, twist it, and use with it the pair from hole 6 to make honeycomb at 7, then leave. Work the second and third pairs together in whole stitch, twist the outer pair twice and work them with the edge pair in order to make the purl at *A*, as described on page 26 of General Notes. Work back again, passing the gimp through it and twisting it, use it with the pair from hole 7. Make honeycomb at 8 and leave. Again, take the third pair from the left as before out in order to make the purl at *B*, working back and making the next honeycomb at 9, then leave. Continue this method until purl at *D* and the honeycomb at 11 are finished. The edge pair and only two passive pairs should remain outside the gimp.

Take the left pair from 11 out to the edge, make purl at *E*, work back, passing the gimp through leaders and leaving them twisted for honeycomb.

Now work the short row of honeycomb. Use the pairs from 6 and 7 for hole 12, those for 8 and 9 for hole 13, and those from 10 and 11 for hole 14. Also, work hole 15 with pairs from 14 and the twisted pair hanging next, which has passed from the outer edge. The outer pair are taken out again to work the purl *F* and brought back again, then used with the pair from 15 for the honeycomb at 16. They once more go out and work the purl *G* and return, and are left twisted ready for honeycomb.

Next work the long row of honeycomb, 17 to 21. The pairs from 12 and 5 work hole 17. Those from 12 and 7 are used for 18, and so on. Next, bring the right-hand gimp through the next five pairs from this honeycomb, and twist each pair ready for the ground net.

Return to the foot side and make the fourth row of ground net (11 holes). Pass the gimp through the end pair, use the end pair

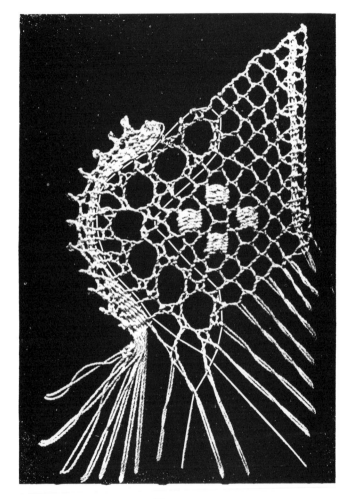

FIG. 171

with the next pair (from 21) to make honeycomb at 22. Work honeycomb at 23 with pairs from 16 and 22 and honeycomb 24 with pair from 23 and the twisted pair next, which has come from the outside.

Take the left-hand pair from 24 out to work the purl *H*, after which they work back through one pair only and left hanging as third pair.

Next work the fifth, sixth, seventh, eighth, and ninth rows of ground net, making the leadwork spots as indicated.

Bring the right-hand gimp through 6 pairs from ground net, and twist each pair ready for honeycomb. Work the honeycomb at 25 with the pair from 22 and the next pair on the right (coming from net). Continue working honeycomb until 29 is worked. For each hole use a fresh pair from the net and leave the left pair out. After 29 is worked, bring the gimp through the right-hand pair, twist for ground net, and then work the next row of grounding. Pass gimp through the end pair, and using it with the pair from 28, work honeycomb at 30. Bring the gimp through the right-hand pair, twist for ground net, and leave.

Work the tenth row of ground net. Bring the gimp through the end pair, and use it with pair from 29 to work honeycomb at 30. Again, bring gimp through right-hand pair, twist it for ground, and leave.

Work honeycomb at 31 with the pairs from 25 and 26, and honeycomb 32 with the pairs from 27 and 28. Continue the honeycomb, working 33 with pairs from 23 and 24 and for each pinhole use a fresh pair from the short honeycomb row and leave pairs out on the left side. After honeycomb 38 is finished, bring the right-hand gimp through one pair, twist for ground net, and leave.

Bring the left-hand gimp through six pairs. Cross the gimps, and leave.

For the edge purls, take the fifth pair (coming from the honeycomb at 33) out to the edge, make purl at 2. Bring the leaders back through one pair of passives only leaving them hanging as third pair. Take the sixth pair out to the edge for the next purl, leave it also as third pair from end, continue until the purl is made at *M*, and the leaders left as third pair. Twist the tenth pair twice (those from the lowest honeycomb hole), bring the left-hand gimp through it, twist for honeycomb, and leave. Twist the eighth and ninth pairs each twice, make honeycomb at 39, pass the left-hand gimp through

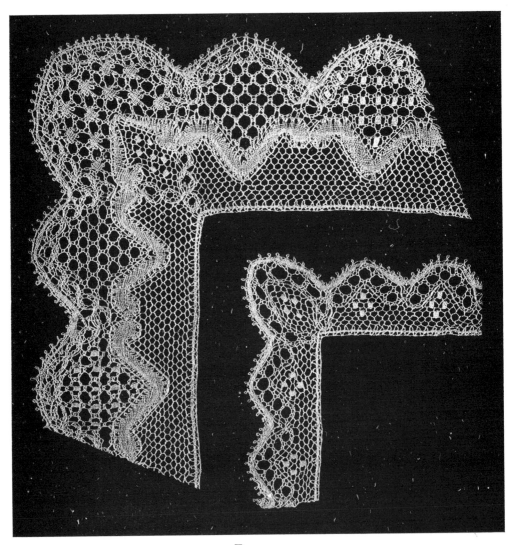

FIG. 172

one pair which twist for honeycomb; the other pair is left to hang as passives.

This completes one head.

Designing Corners (Fig. 172).

It is much more difficult to arrange or design corners to "point ground" than to Torchon edgings, on account of the net ground not being angled at 45 degrees to coincide with the angle of the corner. It will be seen that there is always an awkward little V-shaped space which will not fill in correctly. The only way to overcome this difficulty, is to arrange the design so that it cuts the net ground, right across at the corner. In the corners shown here, both have a little row of honeycomb holes outlined with gimp, running to and from the corner. The actual corner space can then have either net ground or a filling arranged crossways, which not only simplifies the working, but adds strength to the design.

INDEX

ADD bobbins, to, 100
Angles, table of, 145 (Fig. 141)

BARS, and picots, 24 (Figs. 21, 22, 23)
Beds-Maltese corner, 83 (Figs. 93–94)
—— ——, edging, 81 (Figs. 91–92)
—— ——, lace, 76
Blind child's first pieces of lace, 71 (Fig. 74)
—— pin, to work, 98
Blue paper, 10
Bobbin winder, 9
Bobbins, 7
——, coupling, 11
——, gimp, 8
——, handle, how to, 14
——, hanging two pairs from one pin, 14 (Fig. 8)
——, to add, 100
——, to cut off in pairs, 12
——, to wind, 11
——, twisting, 15
Braid, 72 (Fig. 76)
——, dividing into two, 96 (Fig. 103)
Broken threads, 13
Bucks "point ground," 141
—— —— ——, angles to draw, 145 (Fig. 142)
—— —— —— —— ——, another way, 145 (Fig. 143)
—— —— —— ——, on transparent paper, 147 (Fig. 144)
——, cloth, or heavier parts, 148
——, designing corners, 180 (Fig. 172)
—— —— and pattern making, 143
——, "point ground" edging No. 2, 172 (Figs. 167, 168, 169)
—— —— —— —— No. 3, 175 (Figs. 170, 171)
——, fancy holes, and spotted grounds, 149
——, filling "Coat of Mail," 167
—— ——, honeycomb net or, 154 (Figs. 149, 150)
—— ——, honeycomb with plaits, 161 (Fig. 157)
—— —— —— —— another variety, 162 (Figs. 158, 159)
—— ——, horizontal, 166 (Figs. 162, 163)
—— ——, "Mayflower," 165 (Fig. 161)
—— ——, whole stitch honeycomb, 156 (Figs. 151–153)
——, kat stitch, or wire ground, 158 (Figs. 154, 155)
——, filling, kat stitch, spotted, 164 (Fig. 160)
—— ——, pin chain, 160 (Fig. 156)
——, filling, 160
—— ——, for small spaces, 167

Bucks, insertion, No. 1, 169 (Figs. 164, 165, 166)
——, plaits in net ground 154
——, "point ground" table of angles, 145 (Fig. 141)
—— —— —— or trolley net, 151 (Figs. 145, 146)
—— —— —— ——, second diagram, 153 (Figs. 147, 148)
——, purl edge, 150 (Fig. 24)
——, sampler, 143 (Fig. 140)
—— —— key, 142 (Fig. 139)
—— —— stitches, 141
——, sizes of threads, 148

CLOTH stitch, 19
Cluny corner, 80 (Figs. 89, 90)
——, edging, 76 (Figs. 87, 88)
——, lace, 76
Coloured thread diagrams, 18 (Fig. 9)
Cord, 70 (Fig. 75)
Corner Torchon, No. 1, 62 (Figs. 68, 69)
—— ——, No. 2, 65 (Figs. 70, 71)
—— ——, No. 3, 66 (Figs. 72, 73)
Corners, designing Bucks, 180
—— torchon, 60
Cover cloths, 5
Crossing eight plaits or leadworks, 29 (Figs. 28, 29)
—— gimps, 1st method, 97 (Fig. 104, No. 1)
—— —— 2nd method, 98 (Fig. 104, No. 2)
—— —— 3rd method, 98 (Fig. 104, No. 3)
—— six plaits or leadworks, 28 (Figs. 26, 27)
Cutwork, 22 (Figs. 18, 19)

DEMONSTRATION pillow, 18 (Fig. 10)
Double ground, Honiton, 129
—— ——, Torchon, 46 (Figs. 47, 48)
—— picot, 26 (Fig. 24)

EDGE, Torchon, 37 (Figs. 34, 35)
Edging, Torchon for embroidery, 72 (Figs. 77, 78)
——, —— No. 1, 38 (Figs. 36, 37, 38)
——, —— No. 2, 41 (Figs. 40, 42)
——, —— No. 3, 41 (Figs. 41, 42, 43)
——, "nine pin," 74 (Figs. 83, 84)
Egyptian plaited work, 1 (Figs. 1, 2, 3 and Frontispiece)
Embroidery finishings, 70
Enclosing a pin, 15

FILLING, to work a Honiton, 114
Fillings (see Torchon, Honiton, and Bucks)
Five-, six-, seven-, and eight-pin buds, 95

INDEX

"Four-pin bud," 94 (Figs. 101, 102)
Fringe, 72 (Figs. 81, 82)

GAINING on a pin, 99
Getting rid of knots, 101
Gimp bobbins, 8
—— threads, 8, 90, 150
Ground, double, Honiton, 129
——, ——, Torchon, 46 (Figs. 47, 48)
——, twisted half-stitch, 45 (Figs. 46, 47)
——, rose, 49

HALF-STITCH, 21 (Fig. 14)
——, braid, 22 (Figs. 16, 17)
——, plait, 24 (Figs. 21, 23)
——, ——, with single picot, 25 (Fig. 22)
——, reversed, 22 (Fig. 15)
Handle the bobbins, how to, 14
Hanging two pairs from a pin, 14
Honiton backgrounds, 111
——, blind pin, to work, 98
Honiton, braid dividing into two, 96 (Fig. 103)
——, —— stitches, 92 (Fig. 101)
——, curved braid, 98
——, ——, plain hole in, 93
——, clothing, 92
—— filling, a variety of "toad in the hole," 137
—— ——, bars and cutworks, 130
—— ——, "Blossom," 123 (Fig. 126)
—— ——, "Brick," 117 (Fig. 117)
—— ——, "Cartwheel," 115
—— ——, "Cushion," 119 (Figs. 120, 121)
—— ——, cutwork and lattice, 139 (Fig. 138)
—— ——, —— pinhole, 133 (Figs. 134, 135)
—— ——, —— or leadwork, 115 (Fig. 18)
—— ——, —— —— ——, with a hole, 115
—— ——, —— —— ——, —— and a pin, 135
—— ——, —— —— —— —— in a twisted net, 139
—— ——, "Diamond," 115 (Figs. 114, 115)
—— ——, double ground, 129
—— ——, —— —— with cutwork, 130
—— ——, four-pin blocks, 135 (Figs. 136, 137)
—— ——, hexagonal bride, 131 (Fig. 131)
—— ——, "No-pin," 120 (Figs. 122, 123)
—— ——, "Pearl," 127 (Figs. 129, 130)
—— ——, "Pin," 118 (Figs. 118, 119)
—— ——, point d'Esprit, 127
—— ——, swing-and-a-pin, 125(Figs. 127, 128)
—— ——, "Toad-in-the-hole," 121 (Figs. 124, 125)
—— ——, to work, 114
—— ——, whole stitch blocks, 132 (Figs. 132, 133)
—— —— —— —— net and cutworks, 138
——, flower petal, 110 (Fig. 112)
——, gaining on a pin, 99
——, getting rid of knots, 101
——, gimp threads, 90, 97 (Fig. 104)
—— —— —— crossing, 1st method, 97 (Fig. 104, No. 1)

Honiton, gimp threads crossing, 2nd method, 98, (Fig. 104, No. 2)
—— —— —— —— 3rd method, 98 (Fig. 104, No. 3)
——, grounds first Purl pin bars, 111
—— —— second trolly net, 112 (Figs. 145, 146)
—— —— third point d'Angleterre, 113 (Fig. 113)
—— lace, 86
—— leaves, 1. vein of "Mittens," 105 (Fig. 108)
—— ——, 4. raised, 107 (Fig. 109)
—— ——, 5. with serrations, 108 (Fig. 110)
—— ——, 6. raised vein on half stitch, 109 (Fig. 111)
——, picots, and purl edge, 99 (Fig. 24)
——, raised, 106
—— sampler, 88 (Fig. 96)
—— —— key, 87 (Fig. 95)
—— stitches, 90
—— ——, small, 91 (Fig. 100)
—— —— —— key, 91 (Fig. 99)
—— —— —— stitches, 92
——, scroll terminating in a round form, 104 (Figs. 106, 107)
——, setting up, and getting rid of knots, 101
—— sewings, 101
—— ——, double, 103
—— ——, to take an ordinary, 102 (Fig. 105, left)
—— ——, —— —— a top, 102 (Fig. 105, right)
—— sprigs, 89 (Figs. 97, 98)
—— "ten-stick" or stem stitch, 103
—— threads, 90
——, turning stitch, and "ten-stick," 103
——, to add, and take out bobbins, 100
——, to tie out, 101

INSERTION, Bucks "point ground," 169 (Figs. 164, 165, 166)
——, for embroidery finishing, 72 (Figs. 79, 80)
——, —— —— ——, 74 (Figs. 85, 86)
——, Torchon, 44 (Figs. 44, 45)

JOINING plait, or leg, to braid, 27 (Fig. 25)

KAT stitch, or wire ground, 158 (Figs. 154, 155)
—— ——, spotted, 164 (Fig. 160)
Key to Bucks sampler, 142 (Fig. 139)
—— —— Honiton, 87 (Fig. 95)
—— —— small Honiton, 91 (Fig. 100)
—— —— Torchon, 33 (Fig. 30)
Knots, 13
——, reef, 13 (Fig. 7)
——, slip, 11 (Fig. 5)
—— weavers, 13 (Fig. 6)

LEADWORK, 22
——, crossing of eight, 29 (Figs. 28, 29)
——, —— of six, 28 (Figs. 26, 27)

183

INDEX

MATERIALS, 5
Mirror, repeating, 60
"Mittens," 94 (Fig. 101)

NEEDLEPIN, 9

PARCHMENT, 9
Pattern, 6
Pillow, 5
—— demonstration, 18 (Fig. 10)
Picot, 24 (Figs. 22, 23, 24)
——, single, 25 (Figs. 22, 23)
——, double, 26 (Fig. 24)
Pins, 9
——, enclosing, 15
—— to put up, 16
Plain hole, 93 (Fig. 101)
—— —— in curved braid, 93
Plait, half-stitch, 25 (Figs. 21–23)
——, raised, 24 (Fig. 20)
——, to join to an edge braid, 27 (Fig. 25)
——, with picots, 25, 26 (Figs. 23, 24)
——, woven, 22 (Figs. 18, 19)
——, crossing of eight, 29 (Figs. 28, 29)
——, —— of six, 28 (Figs. 26, 27)
——, in Torchon lace, 47 (Figs. 51, 52)
Pricker, 9
Pricking board, 9
——, to make a Torchon, 31
——, to repeat by means of parchment, 36
Pull up threads in right position, to, 15
Purl edge, Bucks, 149 (Fig. 24)
—— ——, Honiton, 99 (Fig. 24)

RAISED Honiton, 106
—— —— leaf, 107 (Fig. 109)
—— —— plait, 24 (Fig. 20)
Repeating mirror, 60
Reversed half-stitch, 22 (Fig. 15)
Rose ground or fillings, 49

SAMPLERS, 29
——, Bucks, 143 (Fig. 140)
——, Honiton, 88 (Fig. 96)
——, small Honiton, 91 (Fig. 100)
——, Torchon, 34 (Fig. 31)
Scroll terminating in a round form, 104 (Figs. 106, 107)
"Setting in," 60
"Setting up," 61
—— —— and getting rid of knots, 101
Sewings, to take a double, 103
——, —— an ordinary, 102 (Fig. 105, left)
——, —— a top, 102 (Fig. 105, right)
Sizes of threads, 31, 90, 148
Sliders, 6
Slip knot, 11 (Fig. 5)
"Snatch pin," 95
Spangles, 8
Spider, 46 (Figs. 49, 50)
——, twisted, 47 (Fig. 31)
Spotted grounds, Torchon, 47 (Figs. 44, 45, 51, 52)
Stitch, half, 21 (Fig. 14)
——, reversed, 22 (Fig. 15)

Stitch, to make, 15
——, whole, or cloth, 19 (Fig. 11)
Square borders, to work, 60

TABLE of angles, 145 (Fig. 141)
"Ten-stick" or stem stitch, 103
Threads, 8
——, broken, 13
——, gimp, 8, 90, 151
——, sizes of, 31, 90, 148
——, to pull up into right position, 15
Torchon corners, 60
—— —— No. 1, 62 (Figs. 68, 69)
—— —— No. 2, 65 (Figs. 70, 71)
—— —— No. 3, 66 (Figs. 72, 73)
—— edge, 37 (Figs. 34, 35)
—— edging No. 1, 38 (Figs. 36, 37, 38)
—— —— No. 2, 41 (Figs. 40, 42)
—— —— No. 3, 41 (Figs. 41, 42, 43)
—— ground, 37 (Figs. 34, 35)
—— ——, with two or three twists between pins, 38
—— ——, double, 46 (Figs. 47, 48)
——, rose ground or filling, No. 1, 49 (Figs. 53, 54)
—— —— —— —— No. 2, 50 (Figs. 55, 56)
—— —— —— —— No. 3, 51 (Figs. 53, 57)
—— —— —— —— No. 4, 52 (Fig. 58)
—— —— —— —— No. 5, 53 (Figs. 59, 60)
—— —— —— —— closed check, No. 6, 54 (Figs. 55, 61)
—— —— —— —— —— No. 7, 56 (Figs. 53, 62)
——, ground or filling, No. 8, 57 (Figs. 63, 64)
—— —— —— No. 9, 58 (Figs. 63, 65)
—— —— —— No. 10, 59 (Figs. 63, 66)
—— —— —— No. 11, 59 (Figs. 63, 67)
—— twisted half-stitch, 45 (Figs. 46, 47)
—— —— with two or three twists between pins, 46
—— insertion sampler, 44 (Figs. 44, 45)
—— lace, 31
——, plaits used in, 47 (Figs. 51, 52)
——, pricking, to make, 33
—— sampler, 34 (Fig. 31)
—— —— key, 33 (Fig. 30)
—— —— stitches, 32
—— spider, 46 (Figs. 49, 50)
—— ——, twisted, 47
—— trail, half-stitch, 45 (Figs. 44, 45)
—— ——, whole stitch, 44 (Figs. 44, 45)
To tie out, 101
To take an ordinary sewing, 102 (Fig. 105 left)
—— —— a top sewing, 102 (Fig. 105 right)

WINDMILL, 26 (Fig. 23)
"Winkie" pins, 95
Whole stitch, 19 (Fig. 11)
—— —— braid, 20 (Fig. 13)
—— ——, with edge, 20 (Fig. 25 right)
Woven plait, leadwork or cut work, 22 (Figs. 18, 19)

ZIGZAG holes, 95 (Fig. 101